When Sorrow COMES

When Sorrow COMES

What Can God, You, and Others
Do to Help Cope with Grief?

RICHARD DEW, MD

ARPress
ILLUMINATING IDEAS
EMPOWERING VOICES

ARPress
45 Dan Road Suite 5
Canton MA 02021

Hotline: 1(888) 821-0229
Fax: 1(508) 545-7580

Ordering Information:
Quantity sales. Special discounts are available on quantity purchases by corporations, associations, and others. For details, contact the publisher at the address above.

Printed in the United States of America.

ISBN-13:   Paperback   979-8-89356-259-0
                        eBook   979-8-89356-258-3

Library of Congress Control Number: 2024903319

When Sorrow Comes:

What Can God, You, and Others Do to Help Cope with Grief?

by Richard Dew, MD

"I believe God is all-knowing and all-powerful."

The author, a physician, writes not only professionally about grief but about his own grief relative to his son being murdered and his father dying soon after this. The book is divided into six chapters addressing various aspects of the topic, such as God and grief, helping yourself and others, special circumstances like the death of a child, grief relative to homicide, suicide, and substance abuse, and ways to hold onto faith. It explores what grief is, its stages, and the symptoms within each one while examining why the loss has happened and other existential questions. Taking steps to heal oneself, such as doing activities, being alone, taking care of physical health, attending support groups, and doing rituals, can help. The chapter on helping other grieving people also offers what to do and what not to do.

The author's book is a good, basic look into grief and the process of grief. The advice on how to cope with one's grief and help others to cope is one of the standouts of the book. By writing from his own experiences with the grief process, the author adds special insight into what it is like to go through such loss. He uses poetry and biblical quotes to add to the connection of healing, and there is much pertinent information on ways to cope and heal. The book is written from a Christian worldview, so it may prove especially valuable to Christian believers. Overall, it is a good read and may be helpful to many people.

- The US Review of Books

Much of the time, we lead unthinking, superficial lives. When sorrow comes, we are forced to consider deeper things.

Contents

Introduction

For fifty years, I led a charmed life. As a physician, I had dealt with many tragedies and deaths. I was touched and saddened every time one occurred. I tried to console and help the victims and their families as best I could. But I was personally unscathed. I had little idea what they were experiencing. Nothing truly bad had ever happened to me.

Then I learned what I never wanted to know. I was caring for my father, who had an accelerated case of Lou Gehrig's disease. In three months, he went from being an active, vibrant man to being paralyzed from the neck down. I was managing fairly well until one morning my phone rang at four o'clock. An unfamiliar voice informed me my twenty-one-year-old son, Brad, had been murdered. At that moment, sorrow came like a thunderclap. Six weeks later, my father died.

After a long up-and-down grief journey, I adapted to the devastation of their deaths. I'm different now, but I live a happy, productive life.

My goal in writing this book is threefold:

1. To help those who have lost a loved one to better understand their grief

2. To assist them to navigate their grief journey in such a manner that they may emerge emotionally healthy, spiritually at peace, and personally happy
3. To help those who want to comfort the bereaved to understand what they are experiencing and how best to offer consolation, aid, and relief

From the outset, you should know I write from a Christian perspective. I cannot separate the spiritual aspects from the rest of my life. That said, many of the insights and suggestions have also proven helpful to nonbelievers with whom I have worked.

Much of the content comes from my own personal experience. More comes from conversations with attendees of more than one hundred talks on coping with grief I have given to lay and professional groups. Most comes from the more than four thousand bereaved parents I have dealt with through the Compassionate Friends, an international support group for families whose children have died.

When Sorrow Comes is divided into six sections:

1. What do we need to know about grief?
2. What role does God play in grief?
3. What can I do to help myself?
4. What can we and others do to help grieving people?
5. Special circumstances: death of a child; miscarriage, stillbirth, and perinatal death; homicide; and stigmatized deaths due to suicide and substance abuse.
6. How does God help, and what role does our faith play?

For readers who have lost loved ones, I hope you find this book helpful. For those seeking information, I hope this assists you in helping others.

God bless.

1

Grief

What Is This Thing Called Grief?

At some point, grief and mourning will be a part of most of our lives. But what is grief? What is mourning?

The dictionary says grief is deep mental suffering or distress brought about by a significant loss. Most often, we think of this in relation to the death of a loved one. However, you will see similar reactions to other closely held losses: divorce, loss of a job, breakup of a long-term relationship, a child leaving home, or the death of a beloved pet.

Grief and mourning are often used interchangeably, but there is a difference. Grief is something that happens internally. Mourning is the outward, visible display of our grief. In our society, grief is okay. Do as much of it as you want. Just don't let others know it's going on. Mourning, the outward display of our grief, is frowned upon, if not forbidden. You can cry at the funeral, but two weeks later, when your compassionate leave is up, keep it hidden.

Things were different in the past when the widow wore black for one year. In some traditions, to this day, men wear a black armband for a year.

Why one year? Why not six months? Or two years? The idea was that with the passage of one year, the griever would pass through all the painful reminder days: the birthdays, the anniversaries, the family days of Thanksgiving, Christmas, and Hanukkah, and the special, little remembrance days we all have. Many are shocked when they wake up on the 366th day and find they are no different than they were on the 365th.

If not one year, how long does it take to get over it? You never get completely over it. I like the term *adapt*. You adapt to your life without your loved one. Most people adapt and live productive, meaningful lives. How long does it take to adapt? That varies from individual to individual. It takes as long as it takes, and that is a lot longer than most people think. Good research, however, has found some reliable approximations of adaptation times.

In general, it takes twelve to eighteen months to adapt to the death of an older parent, two to three years in the case of a spouse, and three to six years in the case of a child. These times are often prolonged if the death was unexpected, violent, or a death stigmatized by society, such as suicide, drug overdose, and substance abuse.

There are many losses that may accompany grief.

It's been said that when you lose a parent, you lose a large piece of your past. When you lose a child, you lose much of your future. When you lose a brother or sister, you lose a good bit of both.

When you lose a spouse, you lose a significant place in society. You are no longer a part of a couple, and many social events are geared for pairs, not singles. If you are older, you may face a future alone. If you are younger, you must contend with rearing children alone and finances, especially if the primary earner died. Added to these is the question of dating or remarriage.

The death of a child is covered in chapter 5.

Stages of Grief

When Brad was killed, despite twenty-seven years of medical practice, I had never heard of the stages of grief. This was not part of the curriculum when I was in medical school. I read everything I could find about the grief process. My reading was dominated by the stages of grief, which were adapted from Kubler-Ross's stages of death and dying. Depending on what I read, the number of stages varied from three to twelve.

Compulsive, type A personality that I am, I determined to plow through them stage by stage. I quickly finished *shock* and moved on to *denial*. I soon discovered it wasn't that simple. I often found myself floundering in two or three stages at once.

The concept of stages is a helpful guide but not an absolute. You get an idea of what to expect and a rough estimation of when it is most likely to occur in the grief process. I think it is more useful to think in terms of aspects or symptoms of grief, which tend to occur in a general but not fixed order. You may skip a stage altogether.

There is an old saying about the grief process: "You can't go around it. You can't jump over it. You can't burrow under it. You must go through it."

What follows is a description of six common aspects (stages) of grief. Three (shock, denial, and disorganization) typically occur early in the grief process, one (depression, loss, and loneliness) in the long, painful middle phase, and two (turning

3

point and adaptation) come later as you begin to emerge and edge toward the new person you have become. Remember that you may find yourself with characteristics of two or three aspects at once. You may dwell in one aspect for a short time or not at all. It's very common to fall back into an earlier aspect after you think you've moved beyond it. The important thing is to keep moving at whatever pace you can.

Shock

It all began like a kick in the gut.
Then, like ripples from a pebble, spread
A nauseating numbness. All senses shut
Down, stunned, inert, frozen, and dead.
Out of body, existing, floating, removed,
Hovering, and looking downward at me
As I received friends and those whom I loved
And sat in a daze hearing your eulogy.
Distracted, unhearing, barely aware
Of the world that's around me, I get up each day
And plod through from morning till bedtime, where
I drop to my knees and desperately pray,
    "Please let me stay in this unfeeling void
    And not have to face my life that's destroyed."*

The first thing you experience is shock. You are numb. You don't think, feel, or act appropriately.

Many express it as being in a daze. Others describe it as floating around, watching themselves go about their activities.

---

* Poems in this book are taken from *Rachel's Cry, a Journey through Grief* by Richard Dew.

A friend of mine told me when people came to offer condolences that I was the perfect host. I smiled as I greeted them at the door. I offered them something to eat or drink. They were impressed I was holding up so well. All the while, I was dying inside.

There are usually gaps in your recollection of this time. I recall very little of the first two or three weeks. I do remember the dying inside. I remember a few people's reactions but little of what they said. Everything else remains as brief flash frames of conversations or occurrences. If I were asked to give a coherent sequence of events of this time, I could not.

Many people in our Compassionate Friends group relate wanting to go to bed, pull the covers over their heads, and remain there. Several did just that.

Shock usually lasts several days to several weeks.

Denial

It's just a dream, a nightmare more near.
You can't convince me he'll never come back.
I rode with him there and helped him unpack
When he went to school earlier this year.
Any day he will be driving back home,
Tall tales to tell with a twinkling eye.
No, he hasn't called. He hasn't said why.
It's been so long, but I know he'll come.
Remove all his pictures, don't say his name—
Reminders just make the tears start to flow.
I'll just keep pretending and trying to do
All I can to keep things the same
And not to admit it. For what I know
In my head, my heart can't handle as true.

Denial is not a conscious decision. It is an unconscious disconnect between your heart and your brain. You intellectually know the loved one is gone. You just can't emotionally accept the whole of it at this time. The death of a loved one is often too much to swallow in one bite. You need to take it a little bit at a time.

Denial can be slight. "I just can't believe this has happened. I expect them to come through the door at any time." It can be serious. The bereaved discards all pictures and reminders and refuses to say or listen to anything associated with the deceased.

Much of what is labeled as denial is minor. Usually it is harmless, and often it is helpful. There is no need to rush in determining what to do with your loved one's clothes and other belongings. Much of the time, I think we delay not out of denial but because of a sense of uneasiness some decisions and actions may cause.

For example, for three years Brad always called home from college at 3:00 p.m. on Sundays. After he was killed, I still stayed home on Sunday afternoons. I knew and accepted that he was dead. I knew for certain the telephone was not going to ring. I just felt uncomfortable going out and doing anything. After a month, my unease dissipated.

Some common forms of denial are deemed particularly bad: the parents who maintain their child's room unchanged for months or years, the wife who just cannot part with her husband's golf clubs or pipe, or the husband who cannot bring himself to dispose of his wife's clothes. Most mourners will eventually find some way to resolve their hesitancy in ending something that gave them comfort and pleasure in the past. Some won't.

If they are moving toward full acceptance of their loved one's death and functioning normally given the circumstances, what difference does it make? It seems to me, colleagues, acquaintances, friends, and family are far more distressed by these acts of denial than the actual mourners.

In most cases, denial tends to be short-lived and is the briefest symptom of grief.

Disorganization

> Life whirls around me; nothing stands still.
> A dozen dilemmas diverge in my brain.
> I can find nothing to hold onto until
> I'm sane. The only thing constant is pain.
> Restless, in motion, moving about,
> With wrenching reminders, I pause to weep,
> Keyed up but listless, hyped and worn out,
> Fatigued to the bone, but unable to sleep.
> Why? Why? Why? No one can tell me why.
> If God, my faith and my prayers can't lift
> Me up, is all that I lived by a lie?
> My anchors have broken. I am adrift,
> > Forgetful and frazzled, control all gone,
> > Searching and seeking, helpless, alone.

As the cushioning effect of shock and denial diminish, the bereaved is left with the brutal fact—their loved one is dead. They will never see, hear, or touch them again.

Their thought processes are overloaded. They are preoccupied with thoughts of the deceased and the details of how their death came about. Concentration is difficult.

This happens about the time many must return to work. Most supervisors try to be understanding, but they expect a timely return to a near normal level of productivity.

I returned to my medical practice after two weeks. For several weeks, I had difficulty remembering the names and/or dosages of medications I commonly prescribed. I frequently missed my turn going home and found myself several miles away with little recall of how I got there.

Many women have told me of getting disoriented in the grocery store. They forgot and left their shopping lists at home. Even when they had their lists, they had trouble going in the aisle where their child's favorite cereal or their husband's preferred ice cream was located.

This is a time when major decisions must be made. Settling life insurance or executing the will is doubly difficult when you are distraught and having trouble concentrating. This is often complicated by well-meaning friends and relatives who give tons of conflicting advice.

Insomnia often becomes severe during this period. This may lead to problems with sedatives or alcohol.

Eating disturbances, anorexia or overeating, tend to begin or worsen.

Many people make bad decisions during this stage of disorganization. They quit their jobs, sever important relationships, or simply withdraw from everything.

I worked with one couple who sold their home three weeks after their son was killed in an automobile accident. "There were just too many memories there." Six months later, they were desperate to get their home and those memories back.

Disorganization happens to most mourners to some degree or another. There is little choice except to plod forward. It usually fades or at least lessens greatly in two to three months.

Depression, Loss, and Loneliness

> Through tear-filled pools into darkness staring
> Back at times now dead and gone. What's ahead
> To me seems bleak, I am long past caring,
> In these dreary hours from which sleep has fled.
> Daylight's no better, It seems my eyes
> Selectively filter and screen the light,
> Making gloomy the world, and gray the skies,
> Matching my mood. There's no hope in sight.
> I can barely get up, work is a chore,
> Profound fatigue permeates all of me.
> Still I plod on, I'm not sure what for,
> There's no point or meaning that I can see.
> > Each monotonous day it seems that I
> > Am just marking time until I die.

The next aspect/stage of grief is called by many different names. Whatever you choose to label it, you have entered the longest and harshest period of grief. There is nothing left to cushion you. Shock has worn off. Denial does not work anymore. Many relatives, friends, and acquaintances have drifted away. They don't know what to do or say and can't handle your continual grieving. You are beginning the painful process of learning to accept and live with the fact that your loved one is gone and is not coming back.

Physical and emotional symptoms may become prominent here. Sleep disturbance, with its subsequent fatigue, is common. Combating this with drugs or alcohol can be disastrous. This is addressed more fully in chapter 3. The mortality rate for men in the first two years after the death of a spouse is 30 percent higher than that of nongrieving men. Clinical depression requiring medication and/or psychotherapy is common during this phase.

This whole period seems a repeated process of three steps forward and two steps back.

You're doing pretty well, then you're blindsided by a favorite tune you shared. You hear a voice so familiar it stops you cold until you realize it's not theirs. The person two people ahead of you in the checkout line has the same height, carriage, and hairstyle as your loved one. You break down in the grocery when there on the shelf are their favorite chips you always bought. These and myriad other seemingly little things trigger what many call "grief spasms." You are suddenly plunged back into the searing pain of those first days after their death.

There are numerous, unanticipated, but very real losses we must contend with: in the case of the death of a young adult, the bittersweet pain when their friends begin to graduate, marry, and have children; your plans for happiness with grandchildren who will never be; your plans to travel with your spouse after retirement, to name just a few. You must cope with the special days—days that are never quite the same again: their birthday; your anniversary; the family times—Christmas, Hanukkah, Thanksgiving, Mother's Day, Father's Day, the summer week at the beach.

You must also struggle yearly with the date that looms above all others—the day they died.

Visitations are the one positive occurrence during this period. Researchers have found very few of these happen beyond the first year of the loss. They tend to be totally unexpected. Some occur as incredibly realistic dreams. Usually the lost loved one appears and reassures the griever that everything is okay. Others are more simple dreams with no obvious meaning. Many people have no visible contact but experience an overwhelming sense of presence, detect the odor of the loved one's favorite perfume, have a powerful consciousness of nearness, or feel some other sort of contact. Most of us wish something like this would happen, but wishing doesn't make it so. At least, it didn't for me.

For some, this period of grief may last a few months, but many times it may persist for several years. It takes as long as it takes, but gradually it diminishes and ends.

At this point, many articles on grief insert anger and guilt as the next two stages of grief. I don't see them as stages. If you're going to use the *stage* paradigm, each stage occurs at a certain point in the grief process, followed in rough order by the next stage. Anger and guilt don't lend themselves to this model. They both, however, are present to some degree in most grief experiences. Each may crop up at any point throughout the grief process. Either may persist long after we have adapted to our loss.

Anger

> A tiny larva, it started to grow,
> Gnawing and boring deep in my soul,
> Creating a rot at my core. Anger so
> Subtly spreading, taking control,
> Then lashing out wildly at anyone who
> Crossed my path. Neighbor or stranger, all the same,
> With no logic or reason outward it flew,
> Randomly seeking someone to blame.
> At God and my friends and my family
> And at him who allowed himself to die.

> Then, lastly, I heaped my rage upon me.
> Now from my mirror glare the angry eyes
> Of a stranger I don't even recognize.

At some point in our grief journey, anger will occur. Its focus, intensity, and duration will depend on the circumstances of our loss. It will also depend on the makeup of your personality. How have you managed anger in the past? Do you fly off the handle easily? Do you just choke it down?

There may be legitimate reasons for your anger: the doctor made a mistake; the driver was drunk; the murderer intended to kill; the suicide victim was bullied.

You may feel the loss could have been prevented and are angry it wasn't: I begged him to quit smoking; the doctor told her if she didn't diet and lose weight, the diabetes would kill her; I told him not to ride that motorcycle; we spent our life savings on therapists and rehab, and she still overdosed.

Sometimes there is no clear-cut person or cause on which to place blame: they died in their sleep, and the autopsy showed nothing; they ate right, exercised, didn't smoke or drink, and still developed cancer. You are angry at being in the situation. This never should have happened. It's not fair. If we find no other good source to blame, we blame God.

Anger may play a minor or major role in your grief. It can impede, or prevent, effective grief work. Anger, undealt with, can damage relationships with others or lead to destructive, long-term bitterness.

It's difficult to get anger under control by one's self. Talking with a trusted friend may be helpful, but frequently our friends are unable to handle our anger. Talking with a counselor or therapist is often the wisest course.

Guilt

A father is supposed to shield and protect
His children from harm. Because of this I've
Tortured myself facing the fact
That my child is dead and I'm still alive.
Was it punishment for some long past sin?
Why didn't I warn him? I should have known.
I might have prevented it if I had been
There. At least he wouldn't have died alone.
At rare times when I laugh, I'm full of shame
For having fun. I can easily see
That logically I am not to blame,
But I can't convince my psyche and me.
    In times of reflection I wonder why
    If God can forgive me, then why can't I?

After the loss of a loved one, most people will experience some degree of guilt. This is usually minor and passes quickly. For many, this becomes a major problem and hinders dealing with your grief.

To an objective observer, this guilt often seems unwarranted. To the griever, it makes perfect sense.

These guilty feelings usually arise from a conviction that something you did, or something you didn't do, in some way contributed to their dying.

Much of the time, you are engaged in what I call magical thinking. Magical thinking is the belief that you somehow should have been able to foresee the future and prevent the death: I shouldn't have let him go out that night; I should have made him go to the doctor sooner; I should have known she was on drugs; I shouldn't have allowed him to swim in that lake; I shouldn't have taken her cell phone away.

At other times, you feel guilty about things that didn't contribute to the death but you think you should have done: I didn't kiss him goodbye when he left for work; I didn't say, "I love you," when we ended her last call; I was too busy at work and didn't spend enough time with him as he was growing up.

A loved one dying alone is a source of guilt in many survivors. This occurs most often in cases of overdose, suicide, homicide, and sudden deaths. Survivors are haunted by unanswerable questions. Did they know how much we loved and cared about them? What were they thinking?

I offer my experience after the murder of my son, Brad, as a possible answer. Feel free to dismiss it as the wishful ramblings of a misguided dreamer. Or, you might be comforted, as I was.

He was driving home from work when two thugs selected him at random. A high-speed car chase ensued while they took turns shooting at him. Finally, a single bullet hit him in the chest. He crashed into a house and died shortly thereafter. He was discovered a half hour later.

What was he thinking as he died? Did he know he was dying? Was he frightened? These thoughts ate at me in those early months after his death. A physician friend of mine helped dispel much of my anguish.

He had done an exhaustive study of near-death experiences (NDE). There have been thousands of documented reports of NDEs. They even occur in young children. He told me the hallmark of an NDE is not fear or terror but an overwhelming sense of peace and serenity. "I believe that was the case with Brad," he said. Could my friend prove that was the situation? No. Could I prove it wasn't? No. I chose to believe this is what happened with Brad—that he died in peace. My mind has been at ease since that time.

As the name implies, an NDE happens when someone's vital signs are fading—when they are near death. It seems logical to me, if the process of dying continues to death, the near-death experience becomes a death experience.

Before I ever heard of near-death experiences, I had always said death was not an end but a door—a door to greater vistas, visions, and realities than we ever imagined. Perhaps a completed near-death experience provides the door.

How can you counter concerns like these? Four things might be helpful in dealing with guilt.

First, realize concerning your inability to predict or prevent the death, survivors almost always tend to overestimate their own contributing role—and their ability to affect the outcome.

Second, understand that guilt implies intent. You did not intend for this to happen. To the contrary, you would have done anything to have prevented it. Instead of feeling guilty, you should feel regret. You are profoundly sorry this happened. You regret you could do nothing to prevent it.

Third, try this exercise. Imagine your situation is reversed with your very best friend. They are the one who suffered the loss. Suppose they come to you overcome by guilt. They proceed to go through the same litany of magical thinking about what they did or did not do that contributed to the death.

Would you tell them, "You're right, you should have known, and you should have done something about it."

Of course, you wouldn't.

Why, then, do you cut your friend slack for not averting the death yet hold yourself to the impossible moral standard that you should have known and prevented it?

Fourth, the key to recognizing regret rather than guilt and judging yourself fairly is, in some way, to begin to view your role objectively rather than emotionally—to allow yourself to be a fallible human. With time and effort, you can do this.

If you continue to be hamstrung by guilt, you need to talk with your pastor or another trained professional.

Turning Point

Dawn does not so much break as it happens.
Dark slides into light so slowly my eyes
Adjust without thought, as pink ribbons
Turn to streamers of orange in eastern skies.
So goes my grief with no strident fanfare.
Sadness and grief have been all that I know,
Then, for a brief moment, it is not there.
Imperceptibly then these moments grow,
Until I laugh without guilt. Life's more worthwhile.
I don't feel as compelled to visit the grave.
I can remember some good times and I smile.
There was nothing dramatic, and I have
Had no revelation, no special thing.
I just felt a bit better sometime last spring.

Calling this time in your grief journey a turning point is probably a misnomer. There is no definitive moment, no clear turning point. It creeps up on you.

Sleep comes easier. The empty feeling in the pit of your stomach fades. Laughter occurs naturally, often without being followed by guilt. Occasionally, you can even see some things positively. You are not constantly preoccupied with your loss. You might even go several hours without thinking about it.

You gradually become able to focus on your loved one's life instead of their death. You can remember some good times and smile rather than cry. You tentatively begin to make plans for the future—the very near future at first, but the future still.

You still get blindsided but less often. Flashbacks and grief spasms still happen, many times for no apparent reason. But they are less frequent, don't sink you so deep, and are much shorter.

You are beginning to live again.

Renewal

> Emerging from the maelstrom of grief, you
> Pause and take stock. Like tempered Toledo steel
> Made stronger by passing through fire, I feel
> Quietly confident, transformed and new.
> Life is more vital, death no longer holds fear,
> A gentle calm pervades much that I do.
> I'm wiser, knowing what others can't know,
> Priorities are straight, perspectives clear.
> My wounds have healed. I'm ready to go
> Back into life, seeking people once more.
> Glad that I'm "normal" again, all of them
> Welcome me back, not knowing that, although
> > I may almost seem like I was before,
> > My soul has deep scars and walks with a limp.

With God's help, you have survived and are ready to reenter life.

You are not over it. You never get completely over it. You adapt to life without your loved one. Your focus is on their life rather than death.

You're not back to the normal others wish for you. The old normal is gone. You are normal in a new way.

Many people at this point exhibit several common characteristics:

- They tend to have their priorities straight. They know what is and is not important.
- They tend to be more understanding and empathetic.
- They don't fear death.
- They tend to be more emotional and let their emotions show more easily. For instance, I can't hear the playing of "Taps" without tearing up.
- Many emerge from their grief with a sense of calling to bring something meaningful from their loss. This calling may take the form of volunteer work, helping the underprivileged, ministering to others who have experienced losses, or some other form of service.
- You can grow spiritually from your losses. You can be your loved one's legacy.

2

God and Grief

The Problem of Why

Why did God take my child?

Why would a good and loving God allow a drunk driver to kill the father of my two small children?

Why did God let her die, and her drug dealer live?

Why are there dreadful, tragic situations in the first place? Does God cause them?

When a loved one dies, those left behind almost always ask, "Why?" I did.

But why what? What is it we want to know?

I think there are three *whys* people struggle with.

The first why is a metaphysical and, for believers, a theological why. Why did my loved one die? What purpose in God's overall plan did their death serve? Where does their death fit into the great scheme of things? I gave up on this question quickly. I will never know why in this sense. I can just hope against hope my son's death did serve some purpose. I dropped this why very quickly. Like me, you probably will not receive a satisfactory answer. There is, however, a constructive way to deal with it. I discuss this in chapter 3.

The second why is more personal. *Why me?* We all know people die. It's thrown at us daily in the evening news. Tragedies occur. Illness, accidents, overdoses, suicides, and homicides happen. We say we understand. We would never admit it, but I think, deep down, most of us believe if we're good people, go to church, tithe, pray, and love our neighbors, God will pay special attention and protect us and ours. Why else would we so often say, "It's not fair," when something bad happens. We realize bad things happen to others but not to us. I was jolted unceremoniously out of this why at a Compassionate Friends meeting. Thirty bereaved parents and I were struggling with the loss of our children. For some reason, I asked, "Why me?"

A woman who seldom spoke asked quietly, "Why not you?"

I had no answer.

The third why is the most troublesome. Why would a good, loving God allow evil, pain, suffering, and death in the first place? Thinkers, theologians, philosophers, and common folk have labored with limited success to answer this question for millennia. After Brad's death, I read the entire Bible twice. I read numerous books by people far wiser than I. I was still left wondering, *But why?*

I still don't have the answer to this why. What follows are my thoughts as a layman that helped me through the worst spiritual crisis I have ever faced. I don't vouch for their orthodoxy or even for their accuracy. To me, they seem reasonable.

The Bible is largely silent about this why. Read the book of Job. Job never gets a suitable explanation.

Jesus seems to accept the existence of evil, pain, and suffering without comment. When He was told of some Galileans Pilate had killed, He gave no explanation. He just said, "Do you think these Galileans were worse sinners than all the other Galileans because they suffered in this way? I tell you, no! But unless you repent, you too will all perish. Or those 18 who died when the tower at Siloam fell on them—do you think they were more guilty than all others living in Jerusalem? I tell you, no! But unless you repent, you will all perish" (Lk 13:2–5). He gave no explanations. He used it as an opportunity to call them to repentance.

Remember, Jesus is the one who said, "Blessed are they that mourn," (Mt 5:4) accepting the fact of mourning without elaboration. He is the one who said, "In this world you will have trouble" (Jn 16:33). He is also the one who suffered humiliation, pain, and death at the hands of evil men.

However, throughout his ministry, He provided His presence, help, comfort, and peace to those who mourned and were troubled. After His ascension, He left the Holy Spirit to continue these activities.

The nearest I can find He ever came to an explanation for evil, pain, and suffering is an enigmatic comment found in Matthew 19:3–8. I may be reading too much into it, but it intrigues me. It dealt with the issue of divorce.

> Some Pharisees came to him to test him. They asked, "Is it lawful for a man to divorce his wife for any and every reason?"
>
> "Haven't you read," he replied, "that at the beginning the Creator 'made them male and female' and said, 'For this reason a man will leave his father and mother and be united with his wife, and the two will become one flesh?' So, they are no longer two, but one flesh.

21

Therefore, what God has joined together, let no one separate."

"Why then did Moses command that a man give his wife a certificate of divorce and send her away?"

Jesus replied, "Moses permitted you to divorce your wives because your hearts were hard"[—and here is the comment that intrigues me—]"but it was not this way in the beginning."

I wonder if he could just as easily have said, "Because your hearts were hard, God allowed sin to enter the world. Because your hearts were hard, God allowed pain, and suffering, and disease to enter the world, *but it was not this way in the beginning.*" Food for thought.

It seems to me that the problem of evil, pain, and suffering comes about primarily from three sources.

The first is free will. We are created in the image of God. What is that image? How are we different from a hermit crab, a dog, or a chimpanzee? We can reason. We can speak. We can think both practically and abstractly. We have a sense of the divine. Some animals have a limited ability to communicate and problem-solve, but it remains rudimentary. I think, however, the way we are most like God and different from all other creatures is our freedom of self-determination, our free will. God can do whatever He wants. To a great degree, so can we. It appears our free will is the one thing God allows us to control with little interference. The fact that something bad happens to me does not mean it is God's will. It may be the will of an evil or careless person.

A second source of evil comes from our being fallen creatures. Whether it is due to the original sin of a historical

Adam or each of us individually choosing to be our own god, the result is the same. We inevitably choose to rebel and be our own god and do wrong. Regardless of how it came about, we are a fallen people. We separate ourselves from God. We take His place. *But it was not this way in the beginning.*

Paul says all creation is fallen. Perhaps natural disasters, hurricanes, tornados, and tsunamis are the result of a universe thoroughly saturated with sin. *But it was not this way in the beginning.*

A third source of evil, pain, and suffering is Satan. This is not fashionable to say in our modern, secular, scientific age, but some evils—the Holocaust, 9/11, child predators—are unexplainable except by some satanic force at work. I think we should be careful of dismissing Satan too easily. Jesus took him very seriously.

What Is God's Role in Our Grief?

So far, this has been my attempt to clarify some possible reasons for the existence of evil, pain, and suffering. But what is God's role in our grief? Where is He when we are really hurting? Can He help? Our image of God shapes our perceptions of God's role in answering these questions. Do we see him as the stern, judgmental God of the Old Testament? Does He micromanage the universe, causing every event, large or small, good or bad, to happen?

One view is that God is limited and there is only so much He can do. This is the view of Rabbi Harold Kushner in his best-selling book *When Bad Things Happen to Good People,* written in response to the tragic death of his son. In his view, he seems to say God knows these bad things happen, but He is limited and cannot do much about it. It seems to me the terms *limitation* and *God* are mutually exclusive. Rabbi Kushner sums up his beliefs as follows: "God would like for people to get what they deserve, but He can't always arrange it." (I'm not sure I want what I deserve.) He encourages us to love and forgive God even though He is not perfect. This seems a rather presumptuous role reversal. I don't find his idea of a limited God helpful. However, he had some ideas on dealing with grief that proved to be some of the most helpful I found anywhere. I will discuss this in section 3.

Another belief is God causes everything, good or bad, large or small, to happen in the furtherance of his overall plan. This is the opinion Dr. C. Everett Koop, the former US surgeon general, gives in his book *The Mountain Moved.*

Dr. Koop's son was mountain climbing. A shelf of rock broke, and he fell over a precipice. He landed on a ledge and over a period of several hours slowly died. Dr. Koop felt God moved the mountain and caused his son to fall. He never questioned this because he was convinced this was part of God's greater plan and was at peace with it. As much as I hate to admit it, he could be right. None of us can conceive of even a fraction of God's plan. But it made me angry. If he is correct, God determined for some unknowable reason to murder Brad, and He had two thugs do it for him. If God causes everything that happens, He is responsible for the bad as well as the good—the Holocaust as well as a miraculous healing, 9/11 as well as the work of Mother Teresa.

I don't find the idea of micromanaging, all-controlling God comforting.

There is another way. I cannot vouch for its orthodoxy or even its accuracy, but it got me through the worst spiritual upheaval of my life.

My vision of God is Jesus Christ as revealed in the Gospels.

Jesus told the apostle Philip, "Anyone who has seen me, has seen the Father" (Jn 14:9). He said, "I and the Father are one" (Jn 10:30). In other words, "If you want to know what God is like, look at Me." We don't have to agonize over this point or that. We have four Gospels describing in detail how Jesus (God) acted, thought, lived, loved, and cared for us.

Does God care that my loved one died? Look at Jesus who wept when his friend Lazarus died.

Is God really a God of love? Look at Jesus. He died for us and forgave the ones who killed him.

Nowhere in the Gospels can I find Jesus doing anything mean, hurtful, hateful, or bad. Nowhere do I see him cause illness, pain, suffering, tribulation, or death in order to better someone or teach them a lesson.

Instead, He spent his time healing the sick, comforting the oppressed, and pointing us to God. This is a God who can comfort us and give us peace.

But the question remains. Why do bad things happen?

Free will is a large part of the answer. Free will carries consequences that can be joyful or painful.

Evil people, of their own free will, do evil things. Sometimes even good people, of their own free will, do evil things. Consequently, others suffer. God does not cause this but, for the most part, does not seem to act to prevent it. (We have no concept of how much He might have prevented without our knowledge.)

Many bad things happen where there is no evil intent. People make reckless, irresponsible, or foolish decisions and hurt others or themselves. They drink and drive, they text while driving, they speed, they eat unhealthy diets, and so on.

Sometimes bad things just happen. Accidents happen. Someone slips on the ice and breaks a hip, or gets a brain injury

25

playing football, or the brakes fail, or a small child runs in front of your car, or a flock of birds causes a plane to crash.

I believe God is all-knowing and all-powerful. He knows what's going to happen before it occurs. He can intervene to change or prevent events if He chooses. I believe He intervenes for good more than we will ever know. In most cases, He allows things to proceed according to the laws of nature He created or the free will of His created people. He allows bad things to happen. He doesn't cause them.

I struggle with the idea God causes someone's death to serve a purpose. I don't believe God kills people to teach a lesson. A lesson and profound good may come from someone's death. These usually occur because God stirs some survivors to perform positive, meaningful actions in the deceased's memory.

I think God knew two bad people were going to kill Brad, and He allowed it to happen without intervening. He allowed it but did not cause it. I wish He had chosen differently, but He didn't. It was not His will. It was the will of two evil individuals whom God allowed to exercise their free will.

I believe God wept with me when Brad died.

This is the framework that got me through my son's and my father's deaths. It represented a rethinking of much of what I had merely assumed in the past. In time, I accepted their deaths, and, for the most part, I am at peace.

3

What Can You Do to Help Yourself?

Even the saddest things can become, once we
have made peace with them, a source of wisdom
and strength for the journey that lies ahead.
—Frederick Buechner

From the moment your loved one died, you embarked on a journey, a grief journey. This trip was unplanned and unwanted but unavoidable. It will probably be the most difficult thing you have ever done. Some friends and family will be especially helpful. Much of the time, however, you must navigate on your own.

This section will give you some practical suggestions on how to exit this journey as a normal, healthy, happy individual. There will be setbacks, long stretches of sadness, pitfalls, and times when you want to give up and quit. The key is to keep moving forward no matter what. I found God to be a steadfast companion—willing to listen when others were not, to hold me up when I faltered, and to give me hope when I felt there was none.

Step One

The first and most important thing you must do is to make a conscious decision: "With God's help, I will get through this. I will not let this death destroy my life."

At first, this may seem a pipe dream. But each morning when you wake, repeat, "I will survive no matter what." Whenever you feel like quitting, repeat, "I will survive no matter what."

We handle grief better when we break it into controllable segments. Take it one day at a time and subdivide that day as much as you need. Initially, getting through this day may consist merely of making it from breakfast until lunch, from lunch until dinner, and from dinner until bedtime. Focus on today. Don't skip to tomorrow. Deal with this day, this hour, this minute, this moment.

Don't let others rush you. Don't rush yourself. At first, try to accomplish one thing a day. Keep it simple. Wash one load. Mow the front yard. As soon as you are able, add other activities.

Spend some time alone each day. This is your time. Pray, meditate, read, write in your journal.

Do something social each day. Call a friend, have a friend over for tea and talk, go for a walk with them.

Try to do something physical each day. A brisk walk or jog can burn off a lot of adrenalin and pent-up emotion.

Try to get enough sleep. Insomnia commonly accompanies

grief. Do the simple things first. Develop a bedtime routine: avoid caffeine after lunch, take a warm bath, drink a glass of milk. Continue these measures, but if sleep is still elusive, melatonin and Benadryl are safe. Be careful about prescription medications. Trazadone and mirtazapine are safe and nonaddictive. (See the section on grief and depression for further discussion of medications.)

Grief Work

After my son was killed, I read everything I could find about grief resolution. Every article said you must do your grief work. At seminars and workshops, every speaker said, "Do your grief work." But none of the articles and none of the speakers told me what grief work was or what I was supposed to do. What follows is the most concise description of grief work I could come up with. And yes, you must do your grief work.

Grief work is the painful process of *intentional* remembrance and preoccupation with our dead loved one. If we are to survive this loss intact, we must hold up the image of what was and review it in detail again and again. Study old picture albums, scrapbooks, and memorabilia, even though it hurts. Talk about them with someone willing to listen.

At first, do this in small increments, a little at a time. We need to share our stories over and over. I call this playing my tapes. The death of a loved one is too much to swallow all at once. Each time we share a story about them, we accept a little bit more. I think there is a predetermined number of times we must tell it before we can accept the full reality of our loss. That number varies from person to person. We do not *get over it*. There is no *closure*. We never *let go*, except in time we let go of the need to hurt, for fear we will forget. We will never forget. We adapt* to a new reality.

In short, healing comes primarily through a deliberate process of remembering, reviewing, and sharing. I have found no better place to do this than a good support group. Don't hesitate to consult a counselor if you are stuck or need more help.

One final note, and I speak from experience. I have often seen a newly bereaved person at a support group meeting wilt when a seasoned veteran member says, "You never get over it." In truth, we never get over it, but we don't remain in that world of searing pain of those early months or years. If we do our grief work, the bad things gradually ebb, and the good memories come to the fore. Things that devastated us early on—a song, a poem, a bundle of old love letters, a sock in the back of a drawer, a tattered Valentine—now bring pleasant memories. I call them warm fuzzies. Life will never be what we wanted or expected, but we can live lives full of meaning and happiness.

1. *Heal.* Healing requires little effort on our part. You have a bad laceration. You have it sutured. From that point on, healing happens automatically. All we have to do is keep it clean and not tear out the sutures. But even with the best of care, we are still left with a scar.

2. *Acceptance.* This is the last of Kubler-Ross's stages of grief. This does not seem adequate to me. It's too

---

* One of the reviewers of this book did not like the term *adapt.* He asked me, "What is the purpose of all of this grief work? What are you working toward? What is your goal?" I had an idea, but I did not know a good word for it. I have since discussed this with my support group and others whose opinions I respect. This is a list of their suggestions and my thoughts on each. Pick the one that best suits your goal as you move through your grief.

passive. You can accept something because you have no other choice.

3. *Reconcile.* To reconcile is to settle or resolve. This is a good term. This is a good goal.

4. *Come to terms with.* I like this one and almost used it, but it's a little wordy to write repeatedly.

5. *Adapt.* To adapt is to conform to (come to terms with) a new situation. It implies work. It also implies we are dealing with a new reality; things are not the same. This is the word I chose to use.

Grief Support Groups

I have a confession. For many years, I pooh-poohed support groups. I thought they were for people who could not manage their own problems. This was odd, because I insisted my alcoholic patients attend Alcoholics Anonymous, the quintessential support group. The ones who attended did much better than those who did not.

When my son died, I found I could not manage my own problems. The Compassionate Friends, an international support group for families whose children have died, was a lifesaver for my wife and me. We remain active members to this day, more than twenty-five years later.

Many large churches and numerous hospice organizations have grief support groups. Most attendees at these groups are bereaved spouses. A few bereaved parents attend, but their needs are significantly different. They may be helped, but their needs are usually better served by groups whose activities are directed solely to bereaved parents. There are two major support groups for families whose children have died: The Compassionate Friends (compassionatefriends.org) with more than six hundred chapters nationwide, and Bereaved Parents USA (bereavedparentsusa.org) with more than two hundred chapters.

A grief support group will not fix your problems. It will not help you fix your problems. The problems associated with our loved one's death are unfixable. It will, however, help us adapt to our new reality. My observation has been those who attend a support group, with or without seeing a counsellor, adapt more quickly and more completely than those who choose to go it alone.

Grief support groups help in several ways.

First, they provide a safe place for us to talk about our loved one. One of the major tools in dealing with grief is talking. In large part, we talk ourselves through our grief. After two or three months, it is common for most of our friends, acquaintances, and family to have moved on with their lives. They don't know what else to do. Often, they are tired of listening. We keep saying the same things and asking the same questions.

For us to move toward adapting to our loved one's death, we need to tell our story as many times as it takes. Members of the group will listen to whatever you need to share for as long as you need to share it.

The group shares problems and methods they have found useful in coping with their losses. For instance, a person is distressed and panicky about the impending anniversary of their loved one's death. Members who have already experienced this may describe various things that helped them cope with this. Someone will point out that the anticipation of the day is usually far more stressful than the actual event itself, a fact unknown to the newly bereaved.

Simply observing the others in the group helps us put our

loss in perspective. It's easy to slide into "Woe is me. My loss is worse than anyone else in the whole world." You realize quickly that your loss is bad, the worst thing that has ever happened to you, but so are the losses of the others in the group.

You can't compare losses. How your loved one left you is the worst possible way. I use this example. When your loved one died, it is as if you were given a large rock representing your loss. You are told, "You must carry this rock for the rest of your life." A cancer death might have a spherical rock, a heart attack a pyramidal rock, an auto accident an ovoid rock, a homicide a lumpy rock, a suicide a cubical rock. Each cause of death brings a specific form of rock we must carry. But no matter the shape of the rock, each rock weighs the same. None is heavier than the next.

The group is a safe place to grieve. It's okay to cry. If you do, someone may hand you a tissue or give you a hug, but they will not tell you, "There, there, don't cry." You can express anger at whomever you think deserves it—insensitive friends, the justice system, doctors, lawyers, or even God, and no one will chide you. You can tell of your anger with your spouse for dying and leaving you alone or your child for overdosing, and no one will say, "Tsk, tsk."

One member of our group was terrified she was going crazy and was planning to see a psychiatrist. She had been going outside in the wee hours of the morning and screaming her son's name over and over. Upon hearing this, three other perfectly normal-appearing women confessed to doing the same type of thing. One was doing exactly the same thing. Another did it in her car on the way to work. The last waited until her husband left in the morning, then screamed and beat on the wall beneath her daughter's picture. Over half of the women attending that day had done something similar. Oddly, no men had. Relieved, the woman did not see a psychiatrist.

Some mothers don't wash their dead child's clothes and keep them in a sealed bag to preserve their scent. A person I knew ate lunch daily in a local cafeteria. She talked to her husband throughout the meal. He had been dead three years. She managed a large business and was perfectly normal in all other ways. Many bereaved people visit the grave site and talk with their loved one.

The bereaved do numerous activities that may seem different or downright weird but are perfectly normal for the situation. A support group is a good place to evaluate this.

There is one last noteworthy benefit of support groups. Booker T. Washington said, "If you want to lift yourself up, lift someone else up."

Talking with people who have successfully adapted to their loss reveals their healing was accelerated when they were able to help another griever.

An opportunity to help others is an important possibility in a support group. When you see someone struggling with a problem you coped with earlier in your grief journey, you can help. You can't fix the problem, but you can lend an empathetic ear. You can tell them what helped you. When you assist another surmount a hill you have already conquered, you feel better. I'm not sure why. You just do. If you can incorporate helping others into your grief work, the result is a double blessing. They are blessed; so are you.

There are many like me who have attended a support group for several years. It is not because we are still trying to resolve our grief. Helping others get through the hard times we experienced helps us. We want to pay back the group for what it did for us. Working with the group is our ministry.

There is real value for those in the painful, disabling early stages of grief. In addition to receiving practical assistance, they receive hope. They see encouraging role models who were once as bad off as they and are now positive, happy, normal individuals.

Grief and Depression

When Are Medications Needed?

> The desire to take medicine is perhaps the greatest
> feature that distinguishes man from animals.
> —Sir William Osler, MD

In support of Dr. Osler's assertion, many Americans seem to think that there is a chemical solution for every problem—too fat, take a pill; too thin, take a pill; can't sleep, take a pill; can't stay awake, take a pill; no energy, take a pill; hyperactive, take a pill.

An old but useful model divides depression into two categories: situational depression (SD) and chemical depression (CD). SD involves 75–80 percent of depressed individuals. Studies have shown most recover quite well without medication. On the other hand, CD usually requires medication as part of the treatment plan.

I have given many talks on grief resolution to physicians' groups. I often use the following example.

A woman goes to her physician, stating her daughter was killed in an auto accident six weeks previously, and she can't stop crying. Anyone who has attended a Compassionate Friends meeting knows this is normal and, more often than not, resolves in time. In spite of this and the studies mentioned above, a majority of physicians say they would prescribe an antidepressant then and there—this even before recommending a counselor or support group.

Doctors, in general, tend to overprescribe. A variation of the old adage "If all you have is a hammer, everything looks like a nail" fits here. If all you have is a prescription pad, everything looks like a pill.

Situational Depression (SD) occurs in response to the losses we experience in life: divorce, loss of a job, children moving away, problem children, death of a loved, one for example. You can probably think of many others. You are supposed to be depressed when these happen.

Grief is a form of SD. I think the death of a loved one entails the severest form of SD.

What can we do to help manage SD? The following summarizes the most important cornerstones in coping with grief. Some have been discussed previously.

1. Make a conscious decision that you will survive, no matter what.
2. Talk about and share your loss as often as you need. As a general rule, you talk your way through SD. I found grief support groups invaluable for this.
3. An individual grief counselor is often helpful.
4. Do your grief work. (See previous discussion of grief work.)
5. Get enough rest. Insomnia is a common companion of grief. The old standbys of a bedtime routine and a warm bath are helpful. Use medication for sleep with caution. Avoid benzodiazipines and alcohol entirely. Benadryl, trazadone, and Remeron (mirtazapine) are

safe and nonaddictive but may leave you drowsy the next morning. (See table 1.)

6. Physical activity such as jogging or walking can burn off a lot of pent-up frustration.

7. Eat regularly but watch sugars and sweets. Too much of these can cause swings in blood sugar, which can affect mood and energy levels.

8. Spend some time alone each day. This is your time. Journal, read, cry, meditate, or whatever gets you out of the daily hustle and bustle.

9. Do something social each day. Just as you need time alone, you also need human interaction. It does not have to be big; call a friend on the phone, have lunch with them, or go for a walk with them.

Chemical depression (CD) results from lowered levels of substances in the brain called neurotransmitters, primarily the chemicals serotonin, dopamine, and norepinephrine. An estimated 20 percent of the population is genetically predisposed to CD. Bipolar disease is the most common form of CD. If the neurotransmitter level is low enough, deep, potentially suicidal depression may occur, often for no apparent reason. Those predisposed to CD may do well until something happens that lowers the neurotransmitter level. A classic example is the depression that results from taking certain types of blood pressure medicines or cortisone preparations. The hormones associated with pregnancy and delivery can trigger a chemically induced postpartum depression. More pertinent to the bereaved, the stress of the severe grief reaction and the SD that accompanies the death of a loved one may bring on a CD.

Medications used to treat CD serve to raise the levels of

neurotransmitters in the brain. Unless a near normal level of these is restored, the depression will persist.

Many people are hesitant to take medication for fear of side effects. The newer antidepressants are safe and have few bothersome side effects. Usually their hesitancy is the social stigma many in our society place on mental illness.

To imply that drugs are bad and that if one were only stronger, had more faith or moral fiber, or just worked hard enough, they should be able to overcome their depression is wrong. It makes as much sense to tell a person with an underactive thyroid, who is deficient in thyroid hormone, that if they were stronger or worked harder, they would not need "drugs" (i.e., thyroid medication).

People who have had previous bouts of CD requiring medication or have a strong history of depression in their family are more prone to CD. After the death of a loved one, a person with one previously documented episode of CD has a 30–40 percent chance of having another; with two previous episodes, a 60 percent chance; with three or more, a 75 percent chance.

Many times, it is impossible to differentiate between a severe SD and a CD. A trial of antidepressant medication may be the only way to tell. Unless there is a previous history of CD or a strong family history, I usually wait two to three months before a trial of antidepressants. If needed, there should be some noticeable improvement. Even with a good response, antidepressants may take two to four weeks to begin improving the depression.

I always caution my patients that antidepressants will not make you feel good. They tend to put a bottom to the free-fall depression you may be experiencing. They make you feel more near whatever is normal for you at this particular time. Unfortunately, for the bereaved with CD, that normal is the usual degree of SD that goes with grief. You don't feel good, but you're now in the same boat as the others in your support group. You are now more able to do your grief work and benefit from it.

You need to work closely with your physician determining the medication and dosage you need. Don't be in a rush to stop your antidepressant. Grief is a long process. So is CD. Follow your physician's advice on when and how to taper your antidepressant.

Medication may be a necessary aid to recovery for the significant number of bereaved who develop CD, but they, just like the rest of us, still must use the coping skills they learn in support groups and from counselors. They need to utilize the previous suggestions for dealing with the SD that accompanies the death of a loved one. Medication may be a necessary aid, but it is only one part of the healing process

Table 1

- **Medications to be avoided**—addictive, tend to make depression worse
    - o alcohol (avoid when used as a medication, e.g. for sleep or to ease stress and anxiety and when drunk in larger quantities than previously)
- **Medications to be used with caution**—potentially addictive, may make depression worse
    - o Benzodiazipines—Xanax (alprazalam), Valium (diazepam), Ativan (lorazepam)
    - o Librium (chlordiazepoxide), Klonopin (clonazepam) may be used for short-term relief of anxiety and agitation

- **Newer antidepressants**—nonaddictive, safe, generally have few side effects
  - o citalopram (Celexa), escitalopram (Lexapro), fluoxetine (Prozac), paroxetine (Paxil), sertraline (Zoloft)
  - o duloxetine (Cymbalta), venlafaxine (Effexor)
  - o trazadone (Desyrel), mirtazapine (Remeron), bupropion (Wellbutrin)
  - o Remeron (mirtazapine) and trazadone, often used as sleep aids and are safe and nonaddictive
- **Older antidepressants**—nonaddictive, significant side effects. May aggravate heart or prostate conditions. Used primarily when there is no response to the newer antidepressants.
  - o Elavil (amitriptyline), Sinequan (doxepin), Norpramin (desipramine), Pamelor (nortriptyline)

Nardil and Parnate are a class of antidepressants that can have severe and potentially fatal side effects. They require extreme caution with other medications and diet. Should be used only under the supervision of a specialist familiar with their use.

Writing as Therapy

Most bereaved people talk their way through grief. Expressing pain, anger, frustrations, fears, and hopes to good listeners helps them deal with their grief as they progress toward adapting to, and acceptance of, their loss.

Some are more introverted or have great difficulty talking with others, especially about something as personal as the death of a loved one. Even empathetic friends and accepting support groups prove intimidating.

For these, I have two suggestions.

First, try talking to God. He is always available and ready to listen. I was more at peace after these conversations, even though I received no audible answer.

The second suggestion is to write. This can be helpful for anyone who is grieving but especially for those who struggle sharing with others. Writing is nothing more than talking on paper.

When we try to resolve our problems, difficulties, and worries in our head, they often become a tangled, jumbled collection of random thoughts. Getting them on paper where we can see them helps us deal with them in a more organized manner.

The classic recommendation for the bereaved is to keep a journal or diary. Try to write your thoughts and feelings daily. Record what angered, frustrated, hurt, or saddened you. Note what uplifted or encouraged you, however short-lived.

For a while, you will probably find you write the same things, especially the negatives, repeatedly. Stick with it. Better they are exposed for possible movement toward improvement than left to fester inwardly.

Your journals can be a valuable benchmark that helps you gauge your progress.

Almost a year after my son's death, I was really disheartened. I felt I had made no headway in dealing with my grief. I was looking back through my journal entries, hunting a poem to use in a talk. As bad as I felt, when I read those year-old entries, I saw a guy who was a basket case—far worse off than I was now. Strange as it sounds, this made me feel better.

Journaling can take other forms. The fourteen-year-old daughter of June Gibbs, a member of our support group, was killed in an auto accident. June began writing her a daily letter, describing her problems and how much she missed her. Over time, the entries began to come less frequently. She wrote the final entry ten years later. She eventually gathered her letters and published them in a beautiful, moving book—*Dear Casey* by June Patrick Gibbs.

My wife kept every card or note we received that had some personal note or something about Brad. In those early months when it was so hard to do anything, she sat at the desk in his room and organized them into a memory book. She then had it published and gave copies to friends and family.

The internet can provide a great platform for writing. Some who have trouble sharing their grief face-to-face can converse easily through social media.

We need to express our feelings. We need to tell our story over and over. This helps whether it is addressed to God, a friend, a pastor, a therapist, a support group, an internet friend, or to ourselves in a journal entry.

Writing a Grief Letter

When you lose a loved one, your family, friends, and coworkers want to help. Unless they have experienced a similar loss, most of them don't know how. Even though they haven't the foggiest idea of what we're going through, many think they know exactly what we should do: we should go back to work; we should take some time off; we should see a therapist; we shouldn't see a therapist; we should stay in and rest; we should get out and socialize; we should take some tranquilizers; we should avoid all medicines. A woman in our support group complained, "People just *should* all over me."

What can we do to help them know what we are experiencing and how we feel about it? How can we let them know what to expect from us in our current situation? How can we let them know what we need?

A grief letter may save you a lot of misunderstanding and discomfort.

The following is a sample. Feel free to use as much or as little of it as you want. Modify it in any way you want. Don't use it if it's not your style.

> Dear _____ (family, church family, coworkers, colleagues ...)
>
> Recently my _____ (husband, wife, son, daughter, mother, father ...), _____ (name by which you want them referred to), died. I am devastated by his/her loss. Everything I have read says it will take several months or years to completely adapt to their death.
>
> I am already discovering that grief is messy. I cry a lot. My emotions are erratic. At times I am angry, impatient, or moody, often for no apparent reason. Sometimes I say the same thing over and over. Please realize this is normal and be patient with me. I am sure it will get better with time.
>
> Don't worry about what you need to say or do. You don't need to say or do anything. Just be there. A brief note, a warm smile, a hug can work wonders.
>
> Please feel free to talk about _____ . Say his/her name. Don't be concerned if I tear up when you do. They are tears of gratitude that you remembered him/her. One of my greatest fears is that he/she will be forgotten. I need to

be able to talk about him/her. Being willing to listen is a priceless gift.

Right now, this is the worst thing I have ever had to deal with. But with God's help, I will survive and eventually come to terms with their death. I cling to that knowledge even though there are times when I don't feel it. I know I will not always feel as I do now. I will smile and laugh again.

Thank you for caring about me. Thank you for your concern. Thank you for listening. Thank you for your prayers. Your support is a gift I will never forget.

There are times where similar letters may be helpful. The first Thanksgiving and Christmas were particularly painful for my wife and me. We wrote family, friends, and coworkers a letter saying we emotionally could not participate in the holidays this year. We also said shopping was too much for us and we would not exchange gifts. We requested instead of gifts, they give a donation to Brad's memorial scholarship fund or The Compassionate Friends.

Reading as Therapy

Read and educate yourself about grief. When my son was killed, I read everything I could find about grief. The better I understood grief, the better I coped.

I have always been a reader. There has seldom been a time when I was not reading on something. After Brad's death, I plunged into reading anything I could find dealing with grief. Although as a physician I had dealt with many bereaved patients, I had received no formal instruction on how best to help them.

This book is a compilation of much of what I learned. I benefitted greatly from reading the grief journeys of others. I learned ways they had coped. From their reactions, I learned many of the odd things I was doing were normal for my situation.

Many survivors find it difficult to concentrate long enough to read a complete book. Our Compassionate Friends publishes a monthly newsletter containing brief articles by other survivors describing their experiences—what helped, what hurt, how they coped with specific problems. The Compassionate Friends.org website has access to numerous newsletters and is a good resource for information on grief. Although directed to families whose children have died, you will soon find that much of grief is generic. What helps a bereaved parent is often useful for a bereaved spouse.

Books dealing with grief are scarce and scattered in most bookstores. Centering.org is an online bookstore devoted solely to books and literature dealing with grief. They have a plethora of useful selections.

A grief journey taken alone is perilous. Most of us need input from somewhere outside of ourselves. Reading can be a tremendous asset for this. If reading is not your cup of tea, you should seriously consider a grief support group and/or a grief counselor.

Meaning and Memorials

> Life is never made unbearable by circumstances,
> but only by a lack of meaning and purpose.
> —Viktor Frankl

Earlier, I discussed the *whys* we ask and get no answers. Maybe we are asking the wrong question. Rather than why, perhaps we should ask, "What now?" Given our terrible loss, what now? What are we going to do with it? For me, the answer came from a person with whom, for the most part, I disagree, Rabbi Harold Kushner.

Tucked away near the end of *When Bad Things Happen to Good People* were two or three pages that changed my life. I was helpless, frustrated, and depressed by the meaningless death of my son. I wanted something meaningful to come from his death.

Kushner says when these tragic things happen, they have no meaning. They just happen. Whatever meaning comes from our loved one's death will come from what those of us left behind bring to it.

He goes on to say we will inevitably erect a memorial in memory of our lost loved one. It will be a memorial for good or for evil. If we become a bitter, negative, hurtful individual, that is our memorial. If, on the other hand, we become a more positive, helpful, caring, empathetic person, that is our memorial.

From the time I read this, it became my mantra. I have dedicated my writing, working with bereaved families, and volunteering at a clinic for the uninsured to Brad. This is his memorial.

I am convinced one of the most powerful forces in coping with grief is to do things that bring meaning to us and our loved one's life.

Ask yourself, "Given this terrible thing has happened, what can I do to bring meaning from my loved one's death?" What will be your memorial?

Rituals, Remembrances, and Reminders

What is it about Holy Communion that moves and inspires people as much today as it did two thousand years ago? Why do we get a lump in our throats when we watch a 9/11 memorial service? Why do I get tears in my eyes when I hear the "Marines' Hymn"? Why do these and similar observances move us to remember and resolve to try to better ourselves and our world?

The following is not an exhaustive list but some things I have seen help, comfort, and inspire me and others.

This is a long story about a small ritual that still means the world to me.

Men don't share as easily as women. Many men use action as a coping mechanism. Two of Brad's favorite pastimes were hunting and fishing. Our home was in the country. The surrounding countryside was wooded and contained a large creek. I had taught him to hunt and fish there. He spent many hours watching deer come and go on our property. After he died, I could not sit still. I had to do something. My first project was to build an elaborate salt lick in view of his bedroom window. I mounted a small plaque with a variation of Robert Louis Stevenson's epitaph on it:

Under the wide and starry sky,
Dig the grave and let me lie.
Glad did I live,
And proud did I die,
And I laid me down with a will,
This be the lines you engrave for me,
"In these woods I loved
My soul roams free.
Home is the fisherman, home from the sea,
And the hunter home from the hill."

Several of Brad's friends' parents had contacted us saying their children wanted to see us but, being young and inexperienced in grief, didn't know if they should or not. We sent invitations to them. More than thirty showed up. We had a brief memorial where I read the epitaph and each person placed some corn on the salt lick. Afterward, we had food and spent several hours telling Brad stories. His friends still mention this to us.

Ten years later when we moved away, I could not be sure the new owners would leave the plaque in place. It belonged there where he grew up, so I removed it from the salt lick and nailed it nearby, high in a huge oak tree. The last time I checked, it was still there.

The first Christmas eve after Brad died, my wife and I lit a candle and placed it and a wreath on his grave. We have done this every year since. Many people place a remembrance candle in the window each night during the Christmas or Hanukkah seasons. Others place a lit candle on the table during holiday meals.

Many in my support group derive great consolation from writing a message to their loved one on a balloon and watching as it soars higher and higher.

Our Compassionate Friends group's most attended event each year is a holiday memorial service. We have some inspirational music and readings, share individual, personal, memories, and light a candle in front of a picture of our child.

My church and a nursing home where I worked have a yearly memorial service for the families of those who died during the preceding year. Both are well attended by appreciative grievers.

Many get great comfort from personal projects of commemoration. The two-year endeavor to collect and publish Brad's personal journals contributed more than anything else to my coming to grips with his death. I still read them several times a year. Numerous bereaved people start, and maintain, a memorial charitable or scholarship fund.

The son of a friend of mine was murdered at college. My friend worked for and achieved national legislation for safety on college campuses in his son's memory.

Keep in mind, intentional remembrance is an important part of our grief work. You might want to try one of these or, better yet, develop some of your own rites of remembrance. In addition to producing personal relief and comfort, these rituals, large or small, help bring meaning to our loved one's life.

Many who have not experienced a great loss will not understand. Anyone who has will.

Take Your Time

I mentioned before, be careful about letting others tell you what you should or should not do in coping with grief. There is, however, one bit of advice I give to all bereaved persons with whom I work. I was doing this long before my son was killed.

Don't make any irreversible decisions for one year after the death of a loved one.

Some things must be done quickly: funeral arrangements, legal issues such as life insurance and estate disposition and the like. Most matters don't. As hard as it may be, you must make decisions rationally and thoughtfully. Don't make decisions based on emotions, which during the early stages of grief are jumbled and unreliable. Discussing things with a counsellor, physician, pastor, or a close friend is usually beneficial.

Several people in our support group have expressed regrets about giving away their child's possessions or articles of clothing immediately after their death. They wished they had waited a while longer.

Be careful about quitting your job. You may find you hate going to work. You may even have given some thought to quitting before your loss. In all likelihood, you won't enjoy any job in these tumultuous early times. The depression, anger, and confusion at this point in the grief process are not conducive to learning a new job. Finally, there is no guarantee you will find one.

You and your spouse may have discussed moving closer to your children. This may well be a good choice but one that seldom needs to be made immediately. Be sure you understand what you will be leaving.

I was in family practice for twenty-five years. I looked forward to going to the office every day. Not so after Brad was killed. I could not relate to my patients as I had before and as I knew I needed to. I took my own advice and kept working. Fifteen months later, I had not improved. In fact, I was worse. I left my practice for a field that did not require such close personal relationships. I was more able to devote myself to my medical practice and my grief work. Ten years later, I returned to family practice and loved it as much as before.

These big decisions are tough. But many small, simple ones are also hard: disposing of their clothes and other personal things and memorabilia, cleaning out their room. There is no rush to do even these. They can be done anytime. Wait until you are comfortable with your decision. That may be months, years, or never. That is okay.

Forewarned Is Forearmed

It is inevitable you will be caught off guard by three common questions. This usually occurs early in the grief process. Preparing a response ahead of time may save you unnecessary emotional discomfort or pain. It can also help prevent you from saying something nasty or hurtful that you will later regret.

The people who ask these questions usually are just trying to start a conversation or merely don't know what to say. Be generous and cut them some slack. Most of the time, they mean well.

Remember, people are usually uncomfortable around bereaved people and would rather be somewhere else. I appreciated the daring ones who had the courage to come and say anything, even the wrong thing, to me far more than those who would not make eye contact or who evaded me altogether.

These are the three most common questions:

1. How are you doing?
2. What happened?
3. Do you have children? And the inevitable follow-up, how many?

How are you doing?

This is a legitimate question. You have probably asked it of troubled people yourself. If you are down, depressed, agitated, and having a horrible day, you might be tempted to be completely honest. "I feel awful. I can't sleep. I cry all day. I don't care if I live or die, but thank you for asking." While honest, this reply helps no one and might lose you a friend. It would better to say something like, "I'm having a really rough time. Thank you for asking."

It's a good idea to have rehearsed several answers to better fit your level of coping for that day: "I'm taking it one day at a time; I'm coping. Not great, but I'm a little better."

End each answer with, "Thank you for asking."

Keep in mind, an important part of your grief work is talking and telling your story. Some who ask, "How are you doing?" actually want to know and are open to talking. To this person, you could say something like, "I'm doing the best I can, but it really helps to talk with someone. Would you be open to coming over for coffee and cookies?" This is one way to find helpful listeners.

The second question is "What happened?" This is none of their business. If you are uncomfortable answering, simply say, "I'd rather not talk about it." If they persist and ask again, you should persist and repeat the same answer.

Much of the time, however, it's easier and kinder to give a brief answer without elaboration. He died of a heart attack. She was killed in an auto accident. He drowned.

If they want you to elaborate further, you can fall back on "I'd rather not talk about it."

Remember, it's often helpful to go through the details of the death over and over, and you need a willing listener for this. Realize once you say, "I'd rather not talk about it," they are not likely to ask again.

The third question, "How many children do you have?" applies to bereaved parents. These parents are loath to omit their dead child when listing their children. Avoiding this omission often requires explanations and clarifications that may prove to be awkward and embarrassing for both the asker and the responder. Having a prepared answer can save you much heartache and distress.

This question is usually asked by a new acquaintance. It serves as a conversation starter. We have all asked it.

You meet or are introduced to someone new. Early in the conversation, you are asked "What do you do?" and "Do you have any children?" quickly followed by "How many?"

The answer I'm comfortable with is, "I have two boys. My surviving son is a librarian in Tucson." Many don't even notice and move on to other topics. If they do notice, they have two choices: they can let it slide or ask for more information.

Many people say something like, "I have two here and one in heaven." This does the job but often leads to more questions.

If this is a brief, perfunctory meeting, I try to steer the conversation quickly to something else. If it is someone with whom I'm likely to have frequent contact in the future—a new coworker, a member of a club, church, or organization to which we both belong—I will tell them without elaboration one of my sons died several years ago. This saves them embarrassment of later asking me how my boys are doing.

While you can prepare for these three questions, many upsetting comments will inevitably come your way. (These will be covered in detail in chapter 4.) In the early stages of grief, they may really hurt. Rest assured, this will happen. You can't always have a ready answer or comeback. But you can decide not to get hung up on it. You can decide ahead of time how you will react and how you will behave.

People don't deliberately set out to say inappropriate things. Then why do they? They just do not know what to say, but they feel they have to say something. So they say what they have heard others say. They ramble. They give advice and try to fix the unfixable. They don't realize a hug or a simple "I'm so sorry" does more good than a dozen clichés, platitudes, or misquoted scriptures.

As frustrating as they may be, realize they mean well. They want to help. They want to say the right thing.

When confronted by such a person, I was grateful for them having the concern and courage to be present. I thanked them for being there. After that, I filtered what they said for anything thoughtful or helpful. The rest I deleted quickly. Before the day was over, I tried to forgive them.

4

What Can You Do to Help Grieving People?

We have considered several ways we can help ourselves. But what happens when someone else has incurred the loss?

What can we do when a family member, friend, colleague, employee, coworker, or acquaintance is mired in the morass of grief? For many, this is unexplored territory. We want to help. But how? What can we do? What do we say? What should we not do? What should we not say?

As much as possible, we need to understand what the bereaved are going through. If you have not had a similar loss, you might want to reread the sections on the different aspects and stages of grief. For example, a bereaved friend may not be consciously withdrawing from us. They may just be numb and in shock and unable to respond appropriately.

Suggestions on What Not to Do

These are a few of the more common things people do that may cause pain or harm.

Primum non nocere. First, do no harm. I heard this caution countless times as a medical student and resident. This principle dates to Hippocrates and the Hippocratic oath. Don't do anything to make the situation worse. We must remember this in our attempts to help others deal with the loss of a loved one.

As far as is possible, we must avoid doing or saying anything that will hamper their journey through grief.

We will first discuss the negatives—what can hurt and hinder—then move on to the positives, things that are likely to help.

Don't abandon or avoid them. One of the greatest regrets I hear from the bereaved is how their circle of friends changed after the death of their loved one. Many whom they felt they could rely on disappeared or slowly drifted away. Loneliness makes grieving even harder.

Bereaved spouses often find others in their couples group feel uncomfortable around them. Perhaps they don't know what to do or say. Maybe they are uncomfortable being around someone grieving. For whatever reason, they withdraw.

Bereaved parents have similar experiences. Many friends and acquaintances don't know what to say. As a result, they say nothing and pull back. A common complaint is "They act as if death is contagious." This is especially true of the parents of your dead child's friends. "If it can happen to you, it can happen to me" is a common, unspoken fear.

Don't give unasked for advice. Everyone knows what a grieving person should do: get counselling, don't see a counselor; get out more, stay out of public; go back to work, stay at home;

socialize, and so on. Many times, the griever does not know what they want or need. Neither do you. If they should ask you for advice, keep it simple and answer only the question asked.

Be careful about theology. Often, mourners will ask you, "Why did this happen?"

You don't know. The best answer is, "I don't know." Leave it at that. Sometimes the grieving person is angry at God and says so in no uncertain terms. Remember, God is big enough to take care of Himself. He doesn't need you to defend Him. Don't try to explain or make excuses for God. This is not a good time for theological discussions.

Be careful about quoting scripture. While the message might be absolutely true, it is often misunderstood and counterproductive.

This is usually done in the painful, early stages of grief. The griever may be struggling spiritually and not receptive to pat theological answers. This is exemplified by a personal example.

About one month after Brad's death, a good Christian friend of mine said, "I've found something that I think will really help you." He then opened his Bible and read the account of the death of David's son in 2 Samuel 12:15–22, which ends with David saying, "While the child was alive, I fasted and wept. I thought, 'Who knows?' The Lord may be gracious to me and let the child live. But now that he is dead, why should I go on fasting? Can I bring him back again? I will go to him, but he will not return to me."

"See," my friend said.

I didn't, but I bit my tongue and thanked him. He wanted so much to help, and I'm sure he'd spent hours scouring the Bible to find something he thought would be caring and supportive. I think the message I was supposed to take away was I would see Brad again. I believe this, but the message I took away was,

"He's dead. You'll see him again. Now suck it up and move on." And I could not do that.

Don't put them on the spot. Don't bring up the death in a social situation when the bereaved is present. Just being there may have taken great effort on their part. If they want to talk about it, let them take the lead, not you. Let them be as outgoing or withdrawn as they need. This is especially true in stigmatized deaths such as suicide or overdoses.

Suggestions on What to Do

Prayer changes things. This is an important tenet of many Christians. Unfortunately, it often comes as a hurried afterthought. The first thing we can do for a bereaved person is to pray for them. Pray they may receive help, comfort, and guidance in this stressful time. Pray we will be given the perception to know what to say and do that will assist in bringing them some measure of solace and comfort. Pray we will be given the determination to continue helping for as long as they need it.

Praying with a bereaved person can give them great comfort. Before you do, be sure both you and they are comfortable in doing so.

The next most important thing you can do is to be there. There is nothing you can do in absentia.

A good example is an act of kindness I will never forget. A physician colleague and his wife had lost a teenage daughter to a congenital defect several years before. I knew them, but they were not close friends. Early on the day after Brad was killed, she was our first visitor. She expressed her sympathy and listened to our story. When the crowds of visitors began arriving, she took over without asking. She answered the door and kept a list of who visited. When someone brought food, she took it to the kitchen. She kept a list of who brought what so we knew to whom we should send thank-you notes and return dishes. She did this until late afternoon and then left.

For someone who has little or no family support, you might help make funeral arrangements. You might also help inform friends and family of the death.

A young patient of mine who had become a local police officer called me the day we received friends. She told me there had been a spate of home burglaries while the families were attending the visitation or funeral. She told us she had obtained permission to park her police car in our driveway while we were attending these.

Several of my wife's friends walked with her three or four mornings a week for four months.

These people's actions exemplify an important principle— do, don't ask.

If you tell a bereaved person, "If there's anything I can do, just ask," you will seldom get a request. If you see something that needs doing, do it. If the leaves need raking, if the lawn needs mowing, if the dog needs walking, if grocery shopping needs to be done, do it.

Another important thing you can do is to listen. Grieving persons need to talk and tell their story. Few people are willing to listen, especially when they hear the same things over and over. Silence is okay. Resist the urge to fill every moment with conversation. Let them take the lead in talking. Be patient. Some griefs take months to years to process. Don't limit their time to share and repeat stories. Repetition is a basic factor in grief resolution.

Don't be concerned if they cry, even if they cry a lot. Crying is often therapeutic. Don't try to shush them. A gentle touch or hug is appropriate. Give them a tissue if they need one and just wait it out.

Six to eight weeks after the funeral is a critical time for the newly bereaved. The world has moved on while they are bogged in grief. The reality of the situation has crashed down. Out-of-town relatives have gone home. Remaining family and friends have resumed their lives. Sympathy cards dwindle and disappear. Casseroles have been eaten, and no replacements are forthcoming. The dogdays of grief have come.

A personal note, an invitation for coffee and conversation, brownies, or even another casserole at this time can help more than Prozac.

Notes to a bereaved person serve as compelling reminders they are not forgotten or alone. My personal bias is for personal, handwritten notes rather than emails or text messages. My wife and I never discarded a note or card that contained something personal about Brad or us.

Many people, especially those younger than I, are active on social media. Use your judgment on how to convey your care and concern. The important thing is to convey it and continue conveying it for a long time.

What should you say in your notes?

Always refer to the deceased by name, never as your husband, wife, or child. Survivors cherish personal stories and anecdotes, serious or funny, about the deceased. How much they meant to us and how they affected our lives are powerful messages.

Survivors especially appreciate recovery of past pictures or newspaper articles about the deceased we have found, no matter how long it has been since their loved one's death. They doubly appreciate it when we can relate our memories of the occasion the article or pictures recall.

Notes have significant impact in the immediate aftermath of the death and during the crucial first six-to-eight-week period. Their effect, however, is ongoing. A note on the deceased person's birthday, the day they died, their wedding anniversary, or other significant dates you may know of is a continual reminder that we remember and still care about them and their loved one. After twenty-seven years, my wife and I still receive several notes on the day he died telling us they remember Brad and are thinking of us.

Taking food to the bereaved is a time-honored tradition for good reason. It helps. It says, "I care."

Survivors often are in no condition to grocery shop or prepare food for themselves, much less the horde of people who visit. The stereotypical casserole, brownies, cake, or anything else we might bring will help feed these groups. More importantly, it says, "I care. I want to help."

There is one problem. The first week or so, supply outstrips demand. The refrigerator, freezer, and kitchen cabinets overflow with food. Over the next two to three weeks, it diminishes and disappears. The bereaved still have little ability or motivation to gather and prepare food. A belated prepared dish, even a zucchini casserole, would be welcome.

A special circumstance is the plight of a surviving spouse. Often their need for companionship is as great as their need for food. This is especially true of the surviving male spouse whose cooking skills may be limited to cold cereal, oatmeal, and scrambled eggs.

Sharing food in times of trouble, grief, and sorrow is a ritual of love and remembrance, a reflection of the holy.

Survivors are especially appreciative of those brave souls who freely say their loved one's name and tell stories of their life. This shows us they mattered.

Many are unwilling to say their names or speak of them for fear of making us cry. We may shed a tear or two but not because someone hurt us by reminding us of our loss. Their loss is never far from us. We always remember them. We cry because we are so happy someone else remembered them also.

Even small actions have great meaning for survivors. There's an ancient Jewish custom of leaving a stone when someone visits a gravesite. We have found a small football, coins, and once a tiny teddy bear on Brad's grave. We never knew who left them, but that's part of value of the gesture. Whoever it was remembered Brad.

It's never too late to offer consolation. Grief never really ends, but it becomes softer and gentler. The painful, bitter emotions of early grief ebb and gradually fade. They may briefly erupt from time to time but for the most part are brought forward only by conscious effort. Survivors recall with gratitude and thankfulness others' acts of remembrance no matter how long the loved one has been gone.

I offer the following examples of moving acts of remembrance others gave to my wife and me years after Brad's death. We will never forget them.

Four of Brad's friends named one of their children Bradley. One called my wife from the delivery room and, in tears, told her his wife had just given birth to a daughter whom they were naming Bradley Yvonne. My wife thanked him and told him she thought Yvonne was a beautiful name. "I think so too," he replied, "but we're calling her Bradley." And so they do.

At a writing conference fifteen years after Brad's death, his high school English teacher introduced herself. Each year as an exercise in public speaking, she had her students give a talk teaching the rest of the class something they might not know. When Brad gave his presentation, he plopped an eighteen-pound rockfish on her desk and taught them how to filet a fish. To me, it was like being reintroduced to him. His teacher still uses this as an example of creativity.

Twenty-five years after Brad's death, out of the blue I received a phone call from his high school football coach. He and several of Brad's teammates who had become coaches were at a meeting. "You know," he said, "we spent two hours telling Brad stories. He was an amazing person. We remember him."

I still get choked up when I think of that call.

Prayer, personal notes, food, memories, and stories, whenever they are received, even years later, are things that bring joy and comfort to survivors. This is not an exhaustive list. There are many other ways you can hearten survivors. Use your imagination. Be aware of their needs, no matter how small, and try to ease them. Any help you may render is a valuable service.

> Whatever you did for one of the least of these
> brothers and sisters of mine, you did for me.
> —Mt 25:40

Suggestions on What Not to Say

Cliché Comfort

> I can imagine
> From a past ordeal.
> I've been there before,
> I know just how you feel.
> I'm sure that you
> Think that you do,
> … But you don't.

It must be God's will.
His time had just come.
He's living with God.
God called him back home.
> If your theology
> Is to uplift me,
> ... It doesn't.

This too shall pass.
Soon it will be gone.
Time heals all wounds.
Life must go on.
> I know you believe
> That time will relieve,
> ... But it won't.

Get hold of yourself.
Don't dwell on the past.
Count all your blessings.
Don't be so downcast.
> I know that I should.
> I would if I could,
> ... But, I can't.

In my experience working with bereaved families, more people are hurt, or even harmed, by what others say than what they do. The list of hurtful things people do is relatively short. The list of hurtful things they say is voluminous.

The sad thing is no one sets out to say something hurtful. They mean to say the right thing. They want to help. So how do they get it so wrong?

I think the main reason is they don't know what to say. Not

knowing, they fall back on what they heard others (who also didn't know) say at funerals or wakes.

This is not restricted to lay persons. Professionals get it just as wrong. In fact, the three groups who most upset the families with whom I work in The Compassionate Friends are psychiatrists/counsellors, physicians, and ministers—in that order. These are the very groups who we think would be most skilled in dealing with the bereaved. They complain counselors/psychiatrists "just don't understand." Physicians try to rush them along and paper-over their problems with platitudes or hurriedly prescribed medications. Ministers, on the other hand, generally get good marks until after the funeral when they move on, leaving the bereaved feeling abandoned.

This is verbatim account told by a bereaved mother whose son was killed in an automobile accident: "They put us in the little room where we shivered and shook for almost an hour. Finally, my husband found a nurse and asked couldn't someone tell us something. 'The doctor is busy right now, but I'll have him see you as soon as possible,' she said. Twenty minutes later, a doctor came in. 'I did not treat your son. The doctor who did has left. But he is dead.' Then he left."

I hope this is an aberration, but I have heard many similar stories.

While the following list is extensive, it is not all-inclusive. All the "words of comfort" have arisen frequently among the bereaved with whom I worked. The comments are quotations from actual grievers.

Should. This was discussed in an earlier section. Everyone knows what the bereaved should do, even if they themselves have never suffered the loss of a loved one.

God clichés. For most people, the loss of a loved one is a spiritual crisis. Many, if not most, resent others' interpretations of God's purposes in their loss.

It was God's will. "So you know the mind of God." See earlier discussion of God in grief.

God never gives us more than we can bear. "Would you care to trade places and see how blessed you feel?"

God needed them more than you did. "Does this mean I'm stronger than God?"

God needed another angel for his choir or flower for his garden. No comment.

Selfish, feel-good clichés. People say these in hopes somehow it will help the bereaved improve. Actually, they say these more to ease their own discomfort with the manner in which the bereaved person is grieving, or their discomfort with not knowing what to say.

You're not your old self. "I would love to be my old self, but that's not possible. Your pointing it out doesn't help."

When are you going to get back to normal? "I'll never get back to my old normal. I'm working as hard as I can to develop a new normal."

You've got to get hold of yourself. "I'd love to. Would you please show me how?"

If there's anything I can do, just let me know. See discussion on what to do. Remember, do, don't ask.

Clichés implying forgetting. Bereaved people, especially bereaved parents, fear in time they or others will forget their loved one or significant things about them.

Now you can have closure. Closure is a popular term with the news media and in Psychology 101. Many bereaved parents become irate at the word *closure.* "Closure is for real estate transactions, not the death of a loved one," one mother told me.

You need to … get over it, turn loose, let go, or move on. What the bereaved hear is, "You need to forget."

Discount clichés. Avoid things that minimize or discount the loss.

I know just how you feel. Sometimes this is even said with reference to the loss of a beloved pet. This may be the greatest loss you have ever had, but it is not comparable to the death of a loved one. Even if you have lost a loved one, you don't know just how another might feel. I find it interesting I have never heard this said in a Compassionate Friends group. In a room full of bereaved parents, the nearest they come is to say, "I remember how I felt when I was at the point of grief where you are."

At least … No matter how you end this sentence, you are minimizing the loss.

Life goes on. I have no idea what is meant by this and how this is supposed to help, yet this "comforting" phrase was said to me more than any other. I tried to be gracious, but it frustrated me. At times, it irritated me, and at other times it made me angry. My life was going down the tubes, and the rest of the world was *going on* as if nothing had happened.

Suggestions What to Say

After the preceding section, you are probably hesitant to say anything. The items on the list of what not to say have one thing in common. We are telling the bereaved what we think will help fix them. They are attempts to fix the unfixable. They seldom help, often hurt, and frequently leave the bereaved feeling frustrated or angry.

The most important thing to them is you are there and you care. You can best show your care and concern by being there and simply and sincerely saying four words: "*I am so sorry.*" Say much more, and you risk drifting into a cliché-loaded minefield.

If you wish to say more than *I'm sorry*, use "I" sentences.

I can't imagine how you must feel. This says, "I don't know how you feel, but I'm trying to understand."

I really miss _____. Better yet, tell what you will miss.

I remember when _____, *or I will never forget* _____. Tell a funny or meaningful anecdote.

You don't have to say anything at all. I have very little recall of events of the first week after Brad died. Two things I remember today as vividly as the day they happened.

One of my best friends is always emotionally in control. I had never seen him elated, depressed, or unusually angry. He was the first to arrive at my home after Brad's death was announced at our church. His car roared up our long drive. Seeing me, he exited his car, ran to me, threw his arms around me, and wept uncontrollably. Stunned, I patted him on his back until he stopped sobbing. He then abruptly released me, rushed back to his car, and left.

The other event happened at the burial. Friends lined the path from the car to the gravesite. As we walked up the path, a tearful, dear friend reached her hand to touch my arm as we passed by.

These two poignant episodes are indelibly etched in my memory. They moved me as little else ever has. And not a word was spoken.

One of the most unnerving things I have experienced in my medical career happened not long after I finished my training and entered private practice.

I had a patient, a single mom who had raised three children with no help from the father. Her youngest son was a star basketball player who had just received a scholarship to play at a major university. He and some friends went on a fishing trip across the state on spring break. His boat overturned, and he drowned. They did not find his body for over a month.

I was a naïve young doctor who had never dealt with a problem like this. Throughout my career, I have always been distraught when I was not in control and did not know exactly what I was doing. I did the best I could for her, but I was not in control, and I did not know what I was doing. I did make numerous house calls, but I said many of the things I just cautioned you not to say.

I had seen several drowning victims who had been in the water for long periods. When they recovered his body, I did convince her to let me identify the body. I attended his wake and his funeral. I walked around for several weeks with a hollow feeling in my stomach because of how badly I had botched things.

Eventually, his mother moved across the state. Twenty-seven years later when I left my practice, I received a note from her. It read, *In the absolutely worst time of my life, you were there, and you cared.*

Comforting the bereaved is not as complicated as it seems. You simply need to ignore your doubts and be present. Try to say the right things, but survivors will forgive bumbling behaviors and awkward statements as long your support, care, and compassion are evident.

5

Special Circumstances

The previous discussions about grief, coping, and helping apply to any death of a loved one regardless of age or circumstances.

There are, however, other losses that present additional, unique problems: death of a child, deaths due to homicide, suicide, and substance abuse. Coping with the grief caused by losses from suicide and substance abuse are complicated further by being stigmatized by sizable portions of society.

In each of these deaths, there are distinctive actions that help, and more that hinder, the grief process. Remember, however, there are things we can do that mitigate or aggravate the grief processes of all deaths. These are discussed in detail in chapters 3 and 4. Review these with each of the following discussions.

Death of a Child

The death of a child, at any age, is the greatest loss a parent will ever experience. It doesn't matter if the child was four or forty years old. A part of yourself has been ripped away. Children are supposed to bury their parents, not the other way around.

The survivors go through the same aspects of grief as described in chapter 2, but there are significant differences from the grief associated with the death of a spouse, parent, close relative, or friend. Parental grief tends to be more intense and longer lasting than with the loss of other loved ones.

How Long Does Grief Last?

Shortly after Brad's death, I attended a grief workshop. The speaker began by saying, "I have some good news and some bad news. The good news is you will get through this. The bad news is it will take a lot longer than you think." He was right on both counts.

The three most common causes of death in children are accidents, homicide, and suicide. In most cases, these are unexpected and/or violent, and thus the grief process is prolonged.

Good studies show the typical time it takes to adapt to the death of a child is three to six years. It takes as long as it takes. That varies from person to person.

In general, the grieving process is prolonged if the death was unexpected, violent, or stigmatized by others.

An odd aspect of the passage of time is seen primarily in parents who have survived the death of a child. For most, this loss is the pivotal event in their lives. After the death, many parents begin dating events in their lives from date their child died. My wife and I found ourselves saying things like, "That was two years before Brad died," or, "That was the year after Brad died." We didn't even realize we were doing it. It just crept in unconsciously. In time, we quit saying before or after Brad died and shortened it to "Before Brad" or "After Brad."

This is not something intentionally morbid. It just happens. It seems natural.

I have asked about this with several Compassionate Friends groups. In every case, most parents did the same thing to one degree or another.

From time to time, I have seen some surviving spouses doing a similar thing, but this is less common.

It's Not Hopeless

> "For I know the plans I have for you," declares
> the Lord, "plans to prosper you and not to harm
> you, plans to give you *hope* and a future."
> —Jer 29:11

Hope is a thing with feathers, that flutters in the soul, and sings the song without the words, and never stops at all.
—Emily Dickenson

With the death of a parent, you lose your past.

With the death of a child, you lose your future.

With the death of a sibling, you lose a great deal of both.

With the death of any of these, you may lose hope.

Although hope may be hidden, Emily Dickenson was right; it never stops at all. Early in grief, hope presents a moving target. We may not see it at first. It does not usually manifest itself in a rush but in small increments over time:

I hope I can make it from breakfast until lunch. I hope I can make it from lunch until dinner—and I do.

I hope I can return to work and not break down and cry—and eventually, I do.

I hope I can move away from my child's death and focus on their life—and finally I do.

I hope I can bring some positive meaning from their death—and I do.

I hope someday I will understand. I'm not there yet, but in time I think I will—if not in this life, then in the next.

Guilt, Blame, and Anger

As mentioned in chapter 1, guilt and anger, to some degree, are usually present after the death of a loved one. They are intensified after the death of a child.

If a parent has no legitimate reason for feeling guilty, they often seem to find one. Parents consider their primary responsibility to their children is their care and protection. If their child dies, they feel guilty because to them it is obvious they have failed their most basic duties.

They lapse into magical thinking. *I should have known. If I had known, then I could have, I should have, I would have ...* Should have, could have, would have eat at the survivor, who often feels guilty about or does not care about surviving.

Remember, guilt implies intent or willful neglect. Parents never intended this to happen and would have done anything to have prevented it. The death becomes more bearable if they can successfully transition from guilt to regret. They regret that their child died and would have done anything to prevent it, but that was not possible. Regret still hurts but isn't as erosive and destructive as guilt is.

Anger and blame often become hurtful, damaging consequences of the death of a child. With most deaths, especially that of a child, the survivors feel helpless. In large part, they are helpless. There was no way to prevent it. It makes no sense. If there is someone at fault, someone to blame and be angry with, the death makes some sort of perverted sense. If it makes sense, we can understand it, at least in part. If we can understand, even a little, we feel temporarily in control.

We find it easier to blame and be angry with the doctor, the nurse, the driver of the vehicle, the drug dealer, our spouse, or God than to admit life can be random, haphazard, and indiscriminate. Bad things just happen, many times for no discernable reason. Brooded upon and left unchecked, anger and blame prevent healthy grief and mourning and can become a poison to our soul.

Releasing guilt, anger, and blame is challenging. No matter how justified your reasons for having them, these emotions must be dealt with in order to move on toward final adaptation to your loss. Clutched tightly, nursed, and fretted over, they become serious impediments to successful coping and grieving. Letting them go is largely a matter of the will. You work consciously to give them up. This is easier said than done. If you feel you cannot do it, you should seek help from a trained counselor, pastor, support group, or insightful friend. You may need to work with more than one of these. Prayer for help beyond our own efforts can be decisive. Whatever it takes. It's that important.

You will not realize how heavy a toll guilt, anger, and blaming impose until you are finally able to lay them aside.

Some Ways the Death of a Child Affects a Marriage

To paraphrase Tolstoy, after the death of a child, every marriage is unhappy in its own way. Friends reassure each other by saying, "At least they have each other." Frequently, that is not enough.

This is the worst loss each partner has ever experienced, and it hit them both at the same time. Each expects the other to supply empathy, caring, and support as in past crises. Usually, this is not forthcoming. Neither is emotionally able to do so.

Both grieve differently. The wife may have an overwhelming need to talk about the death and how it is affecting her. The husband may be drowning in grief and in no mood for talking or listening. He wants only to stay busy and try to work it out for himself. He may need to visit the graveside daily, and she can't stand to go there. She cries all the time. He chokes it down and "stays strong for her." To her, his lack of tears shows he obviously doesn't care.

Each feels the other isn't doing it right. Frustration and anger often result.

Many wives find intimacy almost impossible. The husband feels rejected. He has lost not only his child but also his wife.

One finally has a good day and wants to talk about it. The other has had a horrible day and wants only to sit alone and brood.

What can a couple do to minimize these and all the other stresses that come in the wake of a child's death?

Trite as it may sound, they need to communicate. They must share their feelings. Sharing requires attentive, empathetic listening even when it makes you uncomfortable. This is harder than it sounds. Many times, when the wife shares something that's bothering her, her husband's first instinct is to try to fix it. He doesn't realize his wife is not seeking fixing but a sympathetic ear. His second instinct is to become defensive.

One way to promote effective communication is to express as much of your sharing in "I" sentences rather than "you" sentences.

"I looked at some pictures then cried all day."

"I feel so lonely. I need to be hugged."

"I miss her so much."

When you veer off into "you" sentences, they are often perceived as accusatory, even when not meant as such.

I've known several couples who kept personal journals (almost always written in "I" sentences). They allowed their partner to read selected parts of their journal. It's much simpler to edit what you write than what you say. Sometimes when we read, rather than hear face-to-face, what our partner is feeling and experiencing, we understand better. We are not as inclined to try to correct, fix, or make it better. If we think we can handle it, we might ask, "Would you like to talk about it?" If they decline, let it drop.

These suggestions may be helpful. However, they are often not enough. If you and your spouse are having difficulty, it is better to see a good grief counsellor early rather than later.

A modern urban myth that has been widely accepted as fact and taught in many Psychology 101 classes is 80 percent of marriages end in divorce after the death of a child. *This is not true!* The Compassionate Friends commissioned a poll of twenty-five thousand couples who had experienced the death of a child. The divorce rate in this group was actually less than that of the general population. Other studies have confirmed these results.

It Isn't Fair

> For all sad words of tongue or pen, the saddest
> are these, "It might have been."
> —John Greenleaf Whittier

Survivors of the death of a child are assailed by the unfairness of it all. They have constant reminders of what might have been:

their child's friends graduate, marry, have children and careers. These might have been, these should have been for their child also—but they were not.

This haunting sense of "it might have been" is one of the most lingering aspects of grief. It never goes completely away. You think you have put it to rest, and another reminder pops up. Be careful. It can engulf you and make you bitter, resentful, and depressed if you allow it to. You must deal with it. You can't dismiss it, but you can decrease it. How do you do that?

This is what worked for me and for many in our group who took a similar approach. First, I did the basics. I treated "what might have been" in the manner I learned to treat grief. I participated in our grief support group. I talked about my problems. I talked about Brad. I talked about what might have been. I did my grief work. I read everything I could find on coping with grief. In time, my grief became more controllable. My preoccupation with what might have been lessened somewhat but remained my major stumbling block.

The next step helped me adapt to my grief and come to grips with what might have been more than anything else.

I accepted the reality that Brad would never accomplish or enjoy his dreams or the dreams I had for him. But I realized his life could still make a difference. It could still matter. Making that difference would have to come through me rather than him.

I began doing positive things I knew would please him: volunteering at a clinic for immigrants and the uninsured, working with bereaved parents, teaching medical students how to help grieving families, writing inspirational books. Had it not been for him, I never would have done any of these. These are my memorial to him. He has made a difference.

You can help make a difference in your child's memory.

Everyone has some gift. Every support group needs leadership and volunteers. Charitable organizations are begging for volunteers. Numerous bereaved persons have told me the thing that most helped them come to grips with their own grief was to help a fellow struggler with theirs.

I use a metaphor to describe the role grief, and especially the might-have-beens, played and still play in my grief journey.

While Brad was alive, my world was happy, bright, and sunny. When he was killed, my world went dark. A black cloud engulfed me, my mind, and my world as I stumbled forward in a nighttime of grief. As time passed, the clouds and my moods gradually turned from black to gray. Sadness was less but was still all I had. Then one day, a slender ray of sunlit hope broke through. Ever so slowly, the clouds cleared. My life became brighter. Now, most days are sunny and happy. On the far horizon, however, a small black cloud of grief and might-have-beens remains. I seldom notice it. But sometimes a special song, a small boy fishing or playing catch with his dad, or a memory will trigger a spasm of grief that shouts, "This might have been." When this happens, or sometimes for no reason at all, the small cloud grows and darkens the sun. I am again left frustrated and sad.

Fortunately, these episodes are rare and short-lived. The cloud shrinks back on the horizon, and my world is sunny again.

After the death of a child, our world will never be all sunshine, but there can be more sunshine than clouds.

Miscarriage, Stillbirth, and Perinatal Death

Stillborn

With love I conceived and I bore you,
I dreamt of you when I was a child.
As I felt you grow, I adored you,
With your first feeble flutter I smiled.

Happily, I hummed an old lullaby,
While I readied your room and layette.
With bumps and thumps I felt you reply,
Playing percussion in a happy duet.

Each day that passed our future I planned,
Where we would go and what we would do.
We'd take trips to the beach and play in the sand,
And go to the circus, and visit the zoo.

Many joyful days together we spent,
Looking ahead to all that would be.
Quickly you came, and just as quick went,
And the two of us now is just me.

A past that has passed, a future that's gone,
Everyone's back to normal again.
While here I am, lost and alone,
Torn by thoughts of what might have been.

Memories die out like an ember,
I struggle to hold them, and yet,
It's very hard to remember,
When you were not here to forget.

As soon as there is a positive pregnancy test, parents hope to have a healthy, happy baby to love, nurture, and raise. Their thoughts turn immediately to the future. Will it be a girl or a boy? In short order, their imagination runs amok. They are convinced the child will be good-looking, smart, talented, a gifted athlete, and one day just might be president.

Sadly, for many parents, their hopes and dreams are brought to a sudden, unexpected halt. Their child dies from a miscarriage, stillbirth, or perinatal death. I refer to all three as very early infant death.

The grief process in these losses follows many of the aspects or stages discussed in chapter 3. There are, however, several unique circumstances, different even from the death of an older child, that complicate this grief.

The overarching loss in most deaths is the loss of a personal relationship that may have been active many years. In the cases of miscarriage, stillbirth, and perinatal deaths, the pregnancy and the dreams it fostered were the only chance these grievers had to develop any sort of a relationship. They never had the chance to say hello, much less goodbye.

A miscarriage is defined as the loss of a child before the twentieth week of gestation. Between 10 and 20 percent of pregnancies end in miscarriage.

Most occur before the twelfth week. Whether to announce the pregnancy before the twelfth week can be a difficult decision. Delaying making the pregnancy known may avoid some uncomfortable situations should a miscarriage occur, but it can complicate the grief process. Talking and sharing with others can be helpful in coping with grief, but it may be difficult for those who might help to do so when they were unaware of the pregnancy.

Most miscarriages are due to genetic or chromosomal problems, the causes of which are unknown.

A stillbirth is the death of a child the after twentieth week of gestation up to labor and delivery. Most occur after twenty-eight weeks of gestation.

A perinatal death occurs after the twenty-second week of gestation and within the first week of life.

The bond between a pregnant woman and her baby begins with the knowledge of the pregnancy. It grows stronger and more powerful as the child develops. If the infant should die before or shortly after birth, the mother has lost more than a baby; she has lost a part of herself.

By contrast, deep bonding between the father and baby begins in earnest when he sees, touches, and holds his child. This gives some insight into why very early child death seems to impact mothers harder and last longer than for fathers.

When I give a talk on coping with grief to a women's group, I often ask how many have had a miscarriage. Quite a few raise their hands. I then ask, "How many of you received a note or sympathy card?" Very few hands remain raised.

Since they never saw or had any contact with your child, many friends and relatives don't recognize the depth of your loss. They quickly move on. They expect you to also.

Guilt can be a major stumbling block for anybody who has lost a loved one. This is particularly so for those who have miscarriages, stillbirths, or perinatal deaths. *Was I too active? Should I not have had sex? Did I eat the wrong foods? Should I have quit work sooner?* These are almost never the cause.

Very early infant death presents two other problems. Should you name the baby? Should you have a funeral or memorial service? There are no easy or correct answers to these questions. If you feel strongly one way or the other, follow your heart.

If you are uncertain, discuss this with your pastor or spiritual advisor, counsellor, or a trusted friend. Then follow your heart. Whatever you choose, accept you made the best choice you could under the circumstances.

Don't beat yourself up looking back or second-guessing yourself.

The farther a pregnancy progresses, the more stuff you accumulate. If the child dies, you are left with the painful decisions of what to do with it. You may have decorated a room for the nursery. What now? What do you do with the crib, the diapers, the gifts from the baby shower?

Realize there is no need to make an immediate disposition. You might want to put everything into the room intended for the baby or into some other storage area. Give yourself time to stabilize from your loss. When the time seems right, do what seems best to you. Do not let others try to decide for you or push you into a premature decision.

There is a singular tragedy to stillbirths and perinatal deaths. The mother goes to the hospital expecting to go home with a healthy, cuddly bundle of joy. She sees other mothers leaving with their babies. She hears babies crying. Then, during labor, delivery, or shortly thereafter, her world ends. The baby dies. Instead of a newborn, she goes home holding only shattered dreams.

What Can You Do to Help Yourself?

It is with good reason those who have suffered a very early infant death are called "the forgotten mourners." A major problem with very early infant death is the parents often feel the loss is trivialized, minimized, or even ignored. Many times, they are right.

Don't be too quick to fault others who are of little help. They may have real problems empathizing over someone they never knew and likely never saw. How can they understand when you're experiencing something they have never dealt with?

The section on helping yourself in chapter 3 is useful here. You may find the following suggestions specifically dealing with very early infant death to be beneficial. They fall into two categories: those that help in the immediate aftermath of your loss and those coming a little later. To get maximum benefits, it's usually best for both mother and father to work together.

As with other losses, talking helps. So who do you talk to? God is a good place to start. Immediately after being informed of Brad's death, I began praying for guidance and understanding in coping with my loss. I still do.

Especially with very early infant loss, most people don't understand what you're going through. God does. He can handle your anger, frustration, doubts, and questions.

Begin to build memories while they are fresh. These are a few things parents have told me they found helpful.

If possible, see and hold your baby. Don't let yourself be rushed. Take as much time as you need.

Take pictures of your baby. You may not want to view them now, but you will have them for whenever you are ready. If you have a miscarriage and there is no recognizable infant, get a copy of your ultrasound.

Our Compassionate Friends chapter has a memorial service every December. A part of this rite is lighting a candle before your child's picture. I am moved and choke up every time I see a mother light a candle before her child's ultrasound.

You may want to cut and save a lock of your child's hair.

Have the nurse make you copies of the hand and footprints.

If the hospital gives new mothers teddy bears or the little caps the babies wear in the nursery, be sure you get yours. You're a new mother too. You deserve one.

After returning home. you must cope with the isolation that often accompanies very early infant death. You have tended to the immediate needs. How do you handle the long struggle ahead?

If you have a sensitive friend or two who will cry with you or listen without trying to fix you, treasure them and use them. Call on them for as much as they can handle.

You will probably need more help than they can provide. A good grief counsellor can be invaluable. Just be sure they have dealt with parents who have experienced very early infant death.

The grief counselor will probably recommend a grief support group. Even if they don't, I feel you would be helped by one.

Try to find one composed of others who have experienced early infant death. If available, find a group made up of parents with recent losses, some who are farther along in their grief journey, and some who have successfully dealt with the same ordeal and have remained to mentor others such as you.

If there is not a specific group in your area, attend a Compassionate Friends or Bereaved Parents, USA group. Many of these chapters are large enough to have a subgroup of infant loss parents. Even if the group is not large enough to have a special infant loss group, parents who have lost children of any age can still identify with you more closely than someone who has not suffered the loss of a child. Face-to-face contact is best, but there are some excellent online chat groups that are helpful. Several of these are on The Compassionate Friends website.

Parents who undergo very early infant death haven't had

time to form many memories. Hold fast to the ones you have. As soon as possible, begin a memory book of the ones you recall.

Include the happiness, joy, and wonder you had until your pregnancy turned tragic. Jot them down while your memory is fresh. These may be painful now, but they will likely bring comfort in the future. Enter the touching notes, cards, and helpful actions done for you by others.

Try to involve your family and close friends. If they are receptive, tell them how you feel and what you need. You may want to write a grief letter such as the one mentioned in chapter 3.

Use your child's name if you have named them. Encourage others to do likewise. Thank them when they do.

On special days, light a candle in your child's memory.

Don't make any irreversible changes for several months (one year if possible). A short leave of absence may be more advisable than quitting your job. Trying to get pregnant again as soon as possible may not be best choice. You might find it helpful to discuss significant decisions with your counselor or support group. You could be helped by hearing their experiences with good and bad choices they made.

I mentioned earlier one positive attribute of our grief work. In time, the painful events and bad memories of our child's death begin to fade, and the good times come to the forefront. We begin to focus on their lives rather than their deaths. Unfortunately, with very early infant death, the happy, joyful memories ended with the unexpected death. There were few memories and little or no life on which to focus.

Despite this daunting dilemma, your future is not hopeless or predestined to be sad. For a while, it may seem so, but consider this:

Every life, no matter how brief, is important and has meaning. Every life, no matter how brief, can contribute to the betterment of others and the world.

Tragically, your child will not have the opportunity to do their part. But you can do it for them.

In the aftermath of Brad's death, the major factors that helped me emerge as a positive, hopeful, happy individual were my faith, my support group, and doing worthwhile things in his memory. I recommend you consider all three.

Bringing meaning to your child's death through praiseworthy deeds can contribute mightily toward adapting to your loss. A word of caution: don't jump in too quickly. It took me over a year before I could do anything except the very basics of daily life.

When you have progressed far enough with your grief work, begin considering doing something positive in your child's memory. What should you do?

I don't know what your gifts might be, but here are a few thoughts for consideration.

Start small. Your support group is a good place to begin.

When someone in your group shares a problem with which you have made progress, talk with them individually and tell them what helped you or what you did. Write a note to someone who is struggling. Begin to keep a list of what others did that helped you. When the opportunity presents itself, do the same for someone else.

As you progress in coping with your own grief, through your sharing, you can become the inspiration for those in your group who are just beginning their grief journey.

You might even start, or lead, a new group where one is needed.

If you can help one other bereaved parent cope with their

grief through the memory of your loss, your child's death will not be meaningless.

What Others Can Do to Help or Hinder

The helping and hindering things mentioned in chapter 4 are applicable to parents with very early infant death. Remember, a loss is a loss, be it at twelve, twenty, thirty, or forty weeks of gestation, or three, seventeen, thirty, fifty, or seventy years of age. Just because the loss occurred very early does not lessen the pain.

Here are a few specific things that might help a parent coping with a very early child death:

Since they may receive few, a condolence note is always welcome. If accompanied by a rose, it's even more welcome.

If there is a memorial service, attend.

If the child was named, use it.

In the case of a miscarriage, a note on the due date means a lot.

Be a good listener if you can—to both mother and father.

There are some things that are hurtful after a very early child death:

Ignoring the loss or acting as if it is not important.

Some of the worst "words of comfort" are said to these parents (I did not fabricate these.

Many parents have told me these were said to them):

Are you going to try again? How could I know? I'm not over this one.

You can always have another baby. But I wanted this one.

It was probably for the best. Could you please explain how?

At least you didn't get to know him/her. That's what really hurts.

It probably would have died anyway. How can you know?

It would probably have been retarded. No comment.

It's not like it was alive. Double no comment.

Remember, a simple "I'm so sorry" is all you need to say. Your presence and small acts of kindness showing your care and concern are sufficient—if you continue them long enough.

Sudden, Violent, or Stigmatized Deaths

Deaths by homicide, suicide, and overdose are almost always sudden, unexpected, and often violent, three of the major criteria for a prolonged grief. Stigmatization with suicide and substance abuse just aggravates the situation.

An Ordinary Day

It was just another day,
No one special came
Nothing unusual happened.
The evening was the same.
Just an ordinary day
And then the telephone rang.
From that moment on forever,
Everything was changed.

Humanγ

Richard Dew, MD

Homicide

What's Different about Homicide?

In our support group, we encourage people not to compare losses. In whatever manner your loved one died was the worst way. Each type of loss carries its own baggage, be it an accident, illness, suicide, overdose, drunk driver, homicide, or any of the other ways a person may die.

That said, there are some unique problems that face those whose loved one has been murdered. What are some things that are peculiar to murder that make it so hard to deal with? How are we different? What follows is a brief summary of my own personal experiences, observations, and research.

The death was sudden, and it was violent. These two factors alone tend to lengthen the time of grieving. There was no time for preparation—no comprehension that death could come so quickly and in such a violent, degrading, and brutal manner at the hands of another human being. And we never had a chance to say goodbye.

Murder threatens and casts doubts on our entire value system. We treasure life. Deep down, we believe that if we are good people, don't hurt others, and practice our religion, God and life will be fair to us. Murder is a violation of everything we have been taught was right, decent, fair, and to be expected in life. We feel helpless, frustrated, and without hope. What is of value if not life itself? What other parts of our belief systems are false? What else have I been taught that is fraudulent or untrue? We often lose trust and faith in God and in the world as we believed it to be. Much more has died than our loved one.

Murder is intentional. It's bad enough when a drunk driver is grossly negligent and someone is killed, or when a doctor

88

is careless and someone dies, but in both cases, the death was unintended. In case of homicide, someone deliberately decided that our loved one did not deserve to live and proceeded to kill them. Then, in many cases, they discarded them like trash. In my case, the killers were apprehended because they publicly bragged about murdering my son.

Perhaps worst of all, our loved one suffered, and we weren't there to comfort them. We are left to replay in our imagination what physical and mental anguish they may have endured. Did they know they were going to die? What were they thinking? Did they know how much we loved them and wanted to protect them? Were they afraid? My son died quickly. It horrifies me that I take some comfort in that thought.

We are often overwhelmed by an almost uncontrollable rage and a desire for revenge. How many times have you lain awake at night thinking what you would like to do to them? This is the reason many become involved in victim's rights. This is well and good, but a word of caution. I personally know several people who became immersed in the victim's rights movement, which I support. But with each new shortcoming they saw in the justice system, their anger grew. They were so busy nursing their anger they made virtually no progress in their grief in five or six years. Whatever you do, don't let a desire for revenge or frustration with the very real flaws in the criminal justice system impede your grief work. The people I've known who organized their lives around anger and revenge have become shriveled up. The desire for revenge sucks them dry and gives nothing in return.

Other people's reactions hinder our healing. There is a subtle stigma attached to murder, almost as if it were contagious. There are assumptions, either spoken or unspoken: What were they doing there in the first place? Did it involve drugs? Were they were running with the wrong crowd? Some people are frightened by the circumstances—if it happened to you, it could happen to me. Others are frightened by us. They may not be able to understand. Even if they try, they may not be able to handle our anger.

Since there was a perpetrator, the murder was potentially preventable—if the laws were strict and vengeful enough; if the police had been more active in their patrols; if the perpetrator had not been paroled; if only we had been more diligent in our roles as protectors; if only, if only. We subconsciously find it easier to view the murder as somehow preventable, if not by the police then by us, than to admit that life is sometimes random, unfair, and arbitrary.

The media does its part. It's not unusual to see your loved one's body bag on TV or have TV trucks parked at your home. I remember having a microphone thrust in my face and being asked, "How do you feel?" The victim is often revictimized by a prying media.

The murder of a child places almost unbearable stress on the marriage. If one partner is consumed by rage and the other isn't, the normal strains caused by the death of a child are magnified. If both are filled with rage, they may feed off each other, making matters worse. One may become engrossed in the legal system while the other merely wants to go off and cry.

In cases where the murderer is never caught, there is the additional burden of even more injustice. In the tragic event the victim is never found, all the survivors have left are their own worst imaginings.

The Criminal Justice System

Last, but by far not least, we must deal with the criminal justice system. You should be aware of one side note. In the eyes of the justice system, the murder was a crime against the state, not necessarily against our loved one or us. Notice how each session of the trial begins with something like, "The case of the State versus John Doe regarding the murder of _____."

We often feel, justifiably, that we must put our grief on hold. We cannot emotionally deal with both court proceedings and the pain of grief work. Early on, this is probably true, but long term it is the recipe for disaster. The courts may take years, if ever, to run their course. I encourage you to attend a support group and do as much grief work as you can even while dealing with the justice system. I made it a conscious point not to discuss the justice system at Compassionate Friends meetings. I just talked about my son.

Given the anger, the justice system, and the other factors complicating the murder of a loved one, you would be well advised to see a grief counselor in addition to your support group.

I offer my personal method for dealing with the justice system.

There were times when I had a particularly good or bad day, or like a wounded animal, I just wanted to go away and lick my wounds, but there was another hearing, another deposition, another question from the district attorney, another continuance, or another postponement to complicate matters and make them worse.

I found it helpful to develop a split personality. I pigeonholed everything I could related to the pretrial and trial material, and, as best I could, I ignored it and continued with my grief work.

When something arose that I had to deal with, I took it out, tended to it, and pigeonholed it again as quickly as possible.

Once the case comes to trial, our healing is not helped by having to sit in a courtroom and listen to our loved one's murder described in dispassionate detail, or listen as we are told what a fine, upstanding citizen the killer is, or, worse, listen to the killer explain why our loved one deserved to die and tell blatant lies about them, or the defense attorney try to smear their reputation, or watch as their bloody clothing is put on display and entered into evidence.

I close this discussion of the legal system with three purely personal observations.

First, don't expect much from the criminal justice system, and you won't be disappointed.

Second, the pathway to healing does not lie through the courthouse; that's just a necessary detour.

Third, the harshest sentence does not make things any better; it just makes it less bad than a lighter one. Whether they receive death, life, one year, or one day doesn't bring our loved one back.

In summary, what kind of people are we whose loved ones were murdered?

We are angry people.

We are hurt people—hurt from having our dearest possession and our futures ripped from our grasp in a gruesome way.

We are frustrated people—frustrated by the layer of bureaucracy known as the criminal justice system, which often treats us as nonentities with no rights.

We are lonely people—alone in a world where few can understand our particular pain and even fewer are willing to allow us to share our feelings.

But, we are people who have the potential to go on with life and be the sort of people our loved one would want us to be.

We are people who have the potential to be happy and enjoy life again.

We are people who can live the rest of our lives as a living memorial to our loved one, and in so doing, make them proud.

The death of our loved one is the greatest loss we will ever experience, but the next greatest is what dies within us as we go on living, and to a large degree, this is up to us.

What Can We Do to Help Ourselves?

Most of the things that help and hinder mentioned in chapters 3 and 4 came from my own personal experiences dealing with the grief and the courts following my son, Brad's, murder. This is what got me through and helped me emerge as a happy, normal individual. I recommend you study them carefully. Pay special attention to the notes on support groups in chapter 3.

As I mentioned, the major factor complicating grief after a homicide is the legal system.

I will elaborate on a few that may further help those who are currently dealing with the murder of a loved one.

Realize from the first, there is a high probability the legal outcome will not meet all, or even very many, of your expectations.

Don't make your adaptation to your loss dependent on the outcome in the courts.

Do not put your grief work on hold until the trial is over. Ours was an open-and-shut case, and it still took almost two years to complete the trials. As much as possible, keep your grief work separate from the legal proceedings. When I had to attend a hearing or other legal proceeding, I did. Then, as best I could, I set it aside. I continued this practice through two trials and twelve parole hearings.

I prayed. I worked with my support group and a few close friends. I read all I could find about dealing with grief. I wrote.

Be careful and respectful in dealing with the police and investigators. They are overworked and are usually working on multiple cases at once. They want to solve the case.

Expect some foul-ups. We were initially told Brad was killed in a car crash. Twelve hours later, they apologized and told us he had been murdered.

Find out who you should contact for information and when is the most convenient time. Be polite in all your dealings with them. Do not get angry or argue with them. Do not go to the media, even if you think the police are doing a crummy job.

Most cities of any size have a victim's rights advocate associated with the district attorney's office. They are hired specifically to help you. Use them to get information when possible. Ours was very helpful. When we were having difficulty communicating with the investigators, she could usually get our questions answered or tell us who to call. She notified us of all hearings, depositions, and so on. She attended most of them and both trials with us.

What Can We Do That Hinders Our Coping?

The most common hindrance to processing the grief from a homicide is anger and a desire for vengeance. Murder violates all moral, spiritual, and ethical norms. Our loved one has been killed in a gruesome way, and we are helpless to do anything about it. Helplessness engenders frustration and anger.

A word of caution. There are several victim's rights organizations that have done good work in forcing states to consider the rights of the murdered victim's families. I attended one for several meetings. I quit because many of the members were consumed by almost irrational rage. With each new flaw they found in the justice system, their anger grew. In the three meetings I attended, no one ever mentioned anything about how we could work on our grief or get our lives back on track.

Another hindrance is tying our emotional well-being to the trial verdict. What is the proper punishment to compensate for our loved one's life? The murderer seldom gets the punishment we consider appropriate, and we can do nothing about it

But what is appropriate? One year? Five years? Twenty years? Fifty years? Life without parole? Death?

In my case, both killers were convicted of murder and sentenced to life in prison. However, by state law, they were both eligible for parole in ten years less time served before their trial.

I mentioned I attended twelve parole hearings. I did it because it seemed disloyal to Brad not to. Each time, it was like ripping the scab off a sore. For a while, all the grief and pain came rolling back. I kept them in prison for a few more years, but at what price? And it didn't bring Brad back. After the last hearing, I said, "Enough," and I gave it to the Lord. I wish I had done it sooner.

How Can Others Help or Hinder Our Coping?

The main things that will help or hinder those whose loved ones have been murdered are the basics discussed in chapters 3 and 4.

One thing helpers can do is tough but greatly appreciated. They can attend the trial. Several relatives and friends traveled more than five hundred miles to attend both trials with us.

We will never forget their care and concern at a time when we really did not want to be alone.

Murder is so out of the ordinary. People don't understand and don't know what to do or what to say. So they don't do or say anything.

I was a senior member of a staff of 125 physicians at our hospital. They all knew me, and most of them knew Brad. If anyone should know what to say and do when someone dies, it should be a doctor. After Brad was killed, only six of these 125 ever mentioned his death to me.

If you can do nothing else, say you're sorry, but don't ignore them.

Several things are best avoided when someone loses a loved one to homicide.

Don't pry. Don't ask for details not in the newspaper. Where they were shot or stabbed is not something they are eager to talk about. If they need to talk about the circumstances of the case or the murder itself, they will do so without your asking.

Don't put them on the spot. Don't ask, "Have you forgiven them?" I was asked this twice within a month of the murder. What are you going to say? "No," because more than likely you have not, or "Yes," so the questioner can feel better and maybe leave you alone?

Anger is a major component of the grief process for most who have lost someone to homicide. Many people avoid them because they cannot handle their anger. These bereaved do need to vent their anger and get it out. If you can handle it, you can really help. However, don't make it worse. Don't remind them of some other outrage or point out how the police are botching the investigation. It's best to let them rant without comment. If you want to speak, say something such as, "I bet that hurt" or "I can see how that upsets you."

You don't want to egg them on, but don't try to muzzle them either. Telling them not to be angry or to calm down is not usually received kindly.

Suicide

Although we don't talk much about it, suicide is not far from us. It is the tenth leading cause of death in the United States and the second leading cause in those under the age of thirty-four. Because suicides of young people are more widely publicized, we assume it occurs primarily in this group. Contrary to this popular notion, 80 percent of suicide victims are over twenty-five, and 50 percent are over forty-five.

There are twice as many suicides than homicides. Since 2005, military veterans have died by suicide at a steady rate of six thousand per year (sixteen per day).

These are cold, dry statistics, but what about those who are left after the suicide of a loved one? Their loved one's statistics were 100 percent. They are left with a legacy of grief, guilt, stigma, and haunting unanswered questions of *why*.

Why

Survivors of suicide must come to understand and accept what much of society doesn't: suicide victims died of an illness. They didn't die by choice or due to some weakness, character flaw, or sin. They died of the illness of clinical depression. The death rate from clinical depression is greater than many cancers. Reread the discussion of depression in chapter 3. Between 15 and 20 percent of the general population has a genetic predisposition to depression. Witness the strong family histories of people with bipolar disease.

Although depression played a role in a large majority of suicides, other factors were often present. Stressful situations such as job loss, financial difficulties, and marital or relational breakups contributed. CDC found in 2016 nearly one-third of suicides experienced a crisis during the previous two weeks or expected to experience a crisis in the upcoming two weeks. Almost a quarter were dealing with physical health issues.

The evidence that depression is an illness and a major contributor to suicide is overwhelming. The question is, How?

As a person descends into a clinical depression, it is as if they are wearing black-tinted glasses that prevent them from seeing positive things about life. They develop increasing feelings of hopelessness, helplessness, and worthlessness. They see suicide as the only way to escape constant, intolerable emotional pain. They see suicide not so much as an end to life but as an end to constant, unbearable emotional pain.

We understand this regarding continuous, agonizing physical pain. Some states have made it legal for physicians to assist in the suicide of people with insufferable physical pain. Many people don't approve of this but at least understand it. They understand physical pain but not debilitating emotional pain.

Grief in Suicide Survivors

A person who loses a loved one by suicide goes through the same aspects of grief discussed in chapter 1.

Since suicide is sudden, unexpected, and in many cases violent, the duration of the grief process may be significantly prolonged. The survivor, family, and friends are bewildered. They try to make sense of the situation but are plagued by unanswered and unanswerable questions.

Tragically, the survivor may be the one to discover their

loved one after the suicide. Unlike those who lose loved ones to accidents or murder, they are not left to wonder what happened. They witness it.

The victim might have left a note with an attempted explanation or apology. This may leave more questions than it answers.

Death by suicide is complicated by the stigma society attaches to it. Two episodes I was told of exemplify this.

A suicide survivor told me about a former pastor who refused to conduct a funeral for her son because, "He is already in hell, and there is nothing I can do about it." He went so far as to inform the congregation the reason for his decision.

Although this is extreme, many religious groups view suicide as a sin and have admonitions and strictures against it.

Another mother told me she tried to comfort a mother whose daughter was killed in an automobile accident. Her efforts were rebuffed with, "It's not the same. My daughter wanted to live. Your son didn't."

Although neither of these reactions is typical, I have heard similar ones more often than I care to.

Numerous people in our culture refuse to accept suicide as an illness. They see it as a choice. This is reflected by their describing the victim as committing suicide. They would never say someone committed cancer, committed a stroke, committed a heart attack, or committed leukemia.

Saying someone died by suicide is gentler, kinder, and more accurate.

Others assume the suicide must have been due to some dysfunction in the family. Some or several members of the family must be at blame. It's not unusual for several acquaintances to discuss (i.e., gossip about) what the problem might have been. Having experienced this a time or two, it is little wonder survivors may become hypersensitive and begin to see blame and judgment even where there isn't any.

Guilt is a common reaction after a loved one's death from any cause. Review the discussion of guilt in chapter 1. With the added social stigma, this is even more true in cases of suicide.

You feel guilty because in some way it was your fault: you had an argument; you took away their cell phone; you forgot an important event. The list goes on and on. The depressive illness was to blame. You are not omnipotent.

You feel guilty because you could have prevented it. You missed their cry for help. If you'd only gotten them into therapy sooner, they could have been saved. Therapy is important. Psychotherapy and medication can ease the depression and prevent suicide in many cases. However, therapy is not a cure-all. Most people's depressive illness can be controlled. It is common for some people to have therapeutic control for long periods. Sometimes they relapse. Sometimes the relapse leads to suicide.

Early in my medical practice, I had a patient deeply depressed over the death of her son in Vietnam. I saw her every two weeks. The best psychiatrist in town saw her three times a week for psychotherapy and adjustment of her medications. She was in day care eight hours a day, five days a week at our local mental health center. Her cry for help had been heard and was being addressed. She appeared to be doing well. Then one day on the way home from day care, she walked into a lake and drowned herself. Sometimes intensive therapy by excellent professionals doesn't help. Sometimes you can't help either.

You feel guilty because you didn't see it coming. In the above example, neither did we.

Suicidal people are often very adept at hiding their intentions. You are not clairvoyant.

Anger often goes hand in hand with guilt.

Survivors of suicide are angry at their situation. This never should have happened. Your loved one should still be alive. You were helpless to help the situation. You still are.

At times, you are angry at your loved one for leaving you in such a painful manner.

At other times, you are angry with yourself. You are angry at all the things you blame yourself for and feel guilty about.

Sometimes, you are angry at others. They should have noticed something. They should have done something and didn't.

One of the saddest and most painful aspects of suicide is the sense of rejection the survivors are left with. You loved them with all your heart. Wasn't that strong enough to keep them alive? You did everything you knew to help. Didn't they know that?

You are puzzled, confused, and overwhelmed. You wrack your brain trying to make sense of what has happened. *Why? What did I miss?* You struggle with these and other questions. You dread most of them will go unanswered.

The legacy of suicide is full of pain, sorrow, and regrets. With God's help and a lot of grief work, you can accept and adapt to it. You can honor your loved one's life and have happiness and meaning in yours.

What Can You Do to Help Yourself?

1. The first thing you can do is pray. Everyone agrees grieving people are helped by talking to someone who is kind, caring, compassionate, and a good listener. I found God to be all four.

2. Most suicide survivors benefit greatly by seeing a good grief counselor. They can help you understand your loved one's depression and help you work through the

stigma of suicide. They can also help with PTSD, which is common in suicide survivors, especially those who discovered their loved one's body. A counsellor can help you deal with this as well as the sense of rejection and other unfinished issues in your relationship with your loved one. They can also help you manage conflicting reactions of family members.

3. If the first counselor you see doesn't help, keep looking. There is a good match for you somewhere.

4. Because so many people don't understand or have preconceived opinions about suicide, a good support group can be invaluable. A group composed entirely of suicide survivors and their families is usually best. If there isn't one in your area, The Compassionate Friends works nicely if the victim was a child, grandchild, or sibling. Some churches have Grief Share, a biblically based general support group for those who have lost loved ones. Many hospice organizations have grief support groups.

5. Reach out to whatever friends you have who are good, nonjudgmental listeners. Most friends want to help; they just do not know how. Let them know what you need.

6. Understand and accept, in your heart as well as your head, your loved one died of the illness of depression, not a simple choice to die. In the depths of their depression, they made what to them was a logical decision, not to end their life but to end unbearable emotional agony.

7. Understand and accept, in your heart as well as your head, you were powerless to control your loved one's depression or suicide.

8. Do not define your loved one by their suicide. The circumstances of their death do not alter the fact they were loved and their life had value and meaning.

9. Do not define your life by their suicide. You loved them and did all you knew to do for them.

10. If you have spiritual needs, many pastors are trained in counseling. Some larger churches have their own grief ministries. Many have professional counselors.

11. Read and educate yourself about grief and suicide. When my son was killed, I read everything I could find about grief. The better I understood grief, the better I coped.

12. Write a letter to your loved one. (You might want to reread the account of June Gibbs in chapter 3.) Explain your feelings of rejection to them. Forgive them for anything you think needs forgiving. Ask their forgiveness for things about which you feel guilt or blame. Like June, you might just want to maintain contact by sharing your thoughts, feelings, happiness, sadness, or simply the events of an ordinary day with them.

13. Avoid those who hold negative attitudes about suicide, your loved one, or you.

14. One of the most important aids in your healing can come from finding something positive you can do in your loved one's honor. This may be small: talking to others with similar losses at support group meetings; writing helpful, encouraging notes, emails, or postings on social media. Later it might be larger: giving talks about your experiences and what you have learned about suicide and its effects to church, school, or civic groups. There is a public desire, and need, to learn from those with authentic experiences. You can do helpful, meaningful things your loved one never had the opportunity to do.

What Can Others Do to Help?

These people are hurting like any other person who has lost a loved one, no matter the cause. The general helps in chapter 4 apply here also.

1. Learn about suicide. Understand suicide is a result of a disease, depression. Let the bereaved know you recognize this. Avoid terms that stigmatize. It was not a sin. They did not commit suicide; they died by suicide.
2. Do not abandon them. As with most other stigmatized deaths, many people have no idea what to do, so they disappear, even though they want to help. Show up. Say you're sorry. Take a casserole. They need to know you care.
3. Ask them if there is something you can do for them. Often, they don't ask. Do something anyway. Take food. Go for a walk with them. If they have younger children, take them to a movie and give the grievers a break. If they have very young children, babysit. Walk the dog. Use your imagination.
4. Stay in contact for a long time.
5. Ask If they would like to talk. Offer to lend an ear anytime they want to talk or provide a shoulder anytime they want to cry. If they call and say they want to talk, go. You must make good on your offer. If you don't, they seldom ask a second time.
6. Don't ask for information: the means by which they completed suicide, or if they left a note, or whether they suspected anything. This will likely be perceived as prying. It is.

Death from Overdose and Substance Abuse

The Problem

When a loved one dies of any cause, grieving is unavoidable. Grief associated with any death has many common characteristics. These are discussed fully in chapter 1 and should form the core of your grief journey. However, in our culture, death due to addiction, especially drug addiction, is thought to be different from death by any other cause.

At the time of this writing, the United States is in the throes of an epidemic of deaths from opioid overdoses. In our society, there is a common belief addiction is due to character flaws and is a matter of choice. Furthermore, when someone dies and the cause was their addiction, they are perceived as having been a bad person. It's a short step to judging survivors left behind to have in some way been a bad parent, a bad spouse, or a bad sibling.

The medical profession has long considered addiction to be an illness no different from cancer, infection, strokes, and heart disease. No thinking person would consider these to be due to character flaws or choice.

Although far more people die from tobacco and alcohol addiction, they don't appear to be as overtly stigmatized as drug addiction. Perhaps this is because smoking and especially drinking are more ubiquitous and more socially acceptable than drug use. Tobacco and alcohol addicts are viewed as *weak*, as opposed to drug addicts, who are *bad*. Deaths from tobacco and alcohol addiction usually occur after many years of abuse. Their deaths from lung cancer, heart attacks, COPD, emphysema, and cirrhosis are labeled as illnesses. Usually there is no mention of their addiction. Deaths from drug overdoses are always tagged as due to addiction.

This brings us back to the fact that drug addiction is an illness no different from diabetes or anorexia nervosa. Deaths from drug addiction involve no more choice than the deaths of an obese diabetic or a malnourished anorexic patient.

No one sets out to become addicted. In my opinion, most addiction begins in large part from one or more of three reasons.

First, especially in the younger age group, are peer pressure and self-experimentation. This is especially true of alcohol, opioids, and stimulants.

Second is misguided self-medication for stress or depression primarily associated with alcohol or tobacco. Addiction to these are easier since there are no outside restraints. They don't require doctors' visits or prescriptions. Compared to narcotics, they are much cheaper. Ironically, although alcohol temporarily relaxes you, chemically, it is an emotional depressant. Over time, one becomes more depressed, requiring more alcohol for the desired relaxation or transient ease from depression. Some individuals have a genetic predilection for alcoholism, which compounds their risk of addiction.

A third reason is an addiction that begins as legitimately prescribed narcotics for pain management. Although susceptibility to addiction may vary from individual to individual, opioids taken for too long or in too high a dosage often result in addiction.

More potent opiates, such as OxyContin, were promoted as having no addictive potential and flooded the market. When it became clear they were highly addictive, the damage was done. The widespread use of these more potent opiates led to more fatal overdoses.

In response to public demand, the government began

much-needed controls on opiate prescribing. This caused many doctors and insurers to severely curb or discontinue prescribing opiates. Facing increasing difficulty in obtaining and/or affording their opiates, many addicts turned to the streets where opiates were readily available and cheaper. The two cheapest ones were heroin and fentanyl. They are also the deadliest and cause a majority of fatal overdoses.

Regardless of the original cause of the addiction, continued use of tobacco, alcohol, or narcotics is not usually for pleasure but for avoidance of the pain, craving, and other side effects of withdrawal brought on by discontinuance. In large part, this accounts for the abysmal success of rehab efforts for all three. Fewer than 20 percent of rehab patients achieve permanent abstinence. Witness the COPD patient on oxygen who knows he will die if he doesn't quit smoking, but despite his best efforts can't. The same holds for alcohol and narcotics.

Grieving the Death of a Loved One to Addiction

Coping with death of a loved one from addiction is doubly difficult. You go through the same aspects of grief mentioned in chapter 1. Unfortunately, helpers and comforters are not as forthcoming as in losses from other causes. Your grief is complicated to a greater degree by stigma, guilt, and blame.

Many do not view addiction as an illness but a result of character flaws. They see addicts, at worst, as generally bad people or, at best, weak people who should be able to control their actions. They may make little effort to hide these feelings. The word *junkie* is thrown about freely. They blame the victim directly and the family directly or indirectly. (In my experience, most of the blamers have never had direct contact with an addicted person.)

Although not as blatant or as harshly judgmental, a large part of society doesn't understand addiction. They have difficulty seeing it as an illness. They just don't understand. Despite their best efforts, a sense of blame often bleeds through. One of the few studies of blame done by Feigelman (2011) shows 97 percent of blame comments were made in cases of overdose or suicide. This contrasts with 2–3 percent in cases of accidental death and 0 percent in cases of natural death.

Because of the stigma of spoken or implied blame on the part of some and misunderstanding by would-be comforters, guilt looms larger in deaths from addiction and suicide. As a result, the families withdraw and suffer in silence. They are reluctant to talk about the cause of death.

This blunts a major part of their grief work—the ability to talk about their pain, fears, problems, and concerns resulting from the death.

Guilt is present to some degree in almost all grief reactions. Those who lose a loved one to opioid addiction and suicide generally struggle with guilt more than those whose losses were from other causes.

The following are some of the common sources of guilt associated with addiction I have heard at our support group:

1. Guilt at having a sense of relief that their struggle is over. They have seen their loved one's life ruined by drugs. They have seen them go through the pain of detoxification. They have seen them give their all in rehab only to relapse. This may have happened several times. Conversely, they may have seen them refuse rehab and sink deeper into their addiction. They may have seen them go from being a happy, caring, successful person to one primarily concerned with their next fix.

2. They feel the death was in some way preventable and they could have, should have done something to prevent it.
3. There is guilt that they were too hard on them, that they used tough love and locked them out until they sought treatment; or they were too easy on them and enabled them.
4. They feel guilty about things they said in anger or they said and did out of frustration and helplessness in the face of the destructive effects of the addiction on them, the rest of their family, and on the addicted loved one.
5. They feel guilty about feeling embarrassed or even ashamed over the negative perception others have of them and their loved one.

You may have experienced some, or all, of these guilt feelings. Review the section on guilt in chapter 1. You have every right to feel regret but little cause to feel guilty. You would have done anything to help your loved one. You did everything you knew to do. But you could not do it for them. Don't be any harder on yourself than you would be on someone else who has an addicted family member.

Blame follows closely on the heels of guilt—blame of others and blame of self. They feel if they can assign who is to blame for the death, they might understand it better. They might feel less helpless and more in control. There is a danger they may become so engrossed in placing blame they get sidetracked in their grief work.

Blame may take many guises.

There is blame mixed with anger:

1. At the person who introduced the deceased to drugs

2. At the associates who participated in drug use with them
3. At the person who supplied the drugs
4. At the physician who prescribed outlandishly large prescriptions for drugs and the pharmacists who filled those prescriptions without comment
5. At the pharmaceutical companies who downplayed, or denied, the addictive potential of their drugs and who shipped astronomical quantities of narcotic pills to sparsely populated areas (This is a legitimate target for anger and blame and legal action. Fortunately, steps are being taken to correct these abuses.)

There is the blame expressed or implied by others noted previously.

Just as painful is the self-blame felt by the survivor of a loved one's death from addiction. At times, they blame the deceased—for becoming addicted in the first place; for all the pain they caused; for dying.

As it was with guilt, there is little rational validity to these feelings. They serve to disrupt the grief process and must be dealt with.

Since guilt and blame play such large parts in grieving deaths from addiction, most survivors would benefit from a good grief counselor and support group.

I mentioned in chapter 1 how survivors often measure times in their lives dating from their loved one's death. "That was six months after Mary died." "That was the year before John's heart attack."

Deaths from addiction follow a different time pattern, much like that of long-term illnesses such as cancer, leukemia, and HIV. As with others, there is a before they died and after they died. But there is also an in-between, a roller coaster of remissions and relapses: their cancer shrinks; their white blood cell count returns to normal; their pneumonia clears. Our hopes rise for a while, then they are dashed, only to rise again.

The addicted person follows a similar pattern: they go into rehab, attend Narcotics Anonymous, get a job and are drug-free for several days, weeks, months, or even years. Then something happens, some stressful event: they lose their job, their marriage fails, they have surgery requiring opiates for pain control, they become reacquainted with some old drug-using friends. Sometimes they cannot say why. Tragically, they start using drugs again, and the roller coaster resumes. They may have multiple remissions and relapses until the fatal crash occurs.

What You Can Do to Help Yourself

Before reading these suggestions dealing more specifically with losing a loved one to addiction, reread the section on helping yourself in chapter 3.

1. A significant portion of our society holds negative and judgmental attitudes toward addiction. Because of this, those who have lost loved ones to addiction are often plagued by guilt, blame, and shame. If this is a problem with you, seriously consider getting professional counseling for you and possibly your family.

2. For the same reasons, these survivors tend to withdraw and isolate themselves. This deprives them of one of the most important aids in coping with grief, the ability to talk with understanding others about their pain, difficulties, and struggles. A good support group can be lifesaving. A support group consisting of others who

have had losses due to addiction is ideal. Unfortunately, there are not many of these. If the victim was a child (they are still your little boy or little girl regardless of their age), The Compassionate Friends is a good option. Our chapter is not large, but we have five families who have lost a child or an adult child through an overdose. Two of these are long-term members who attend primarily to help others with addiction losses.

3. Accept and internalize the established fact that addiction is a disease, pure and simple. You may have grown up in a culture where addiction was considered a choice or a personal weakness. Subconsciously, you may harbor doubts that addiction is a disease. It is. Accept it. This will go a long way toward putting to rest much of your feelings of guilt and blame.

4. Do not define your loved one by their addiction. The circumstances of their death don't eradicate the fact they were loved, and their life had value and meaning.

5. Accept the circumstances of the death and the part addiction played in it.

6. Talk about your complicated and conflicting feelings and your grief over your loss. Utilize friends who are good, nonjudgmental listeners and your support group. Each time you express your feelings, you take one more small step toward coming to terms with your loss. Voicing your struggles and concerns to your support group not only helps you but also may help others who have had similar experiences but are reluctant to speak.

7. Accept the fact you were powerless to control your loved one's addiction.

8. Avoid those who hold negative attitudes about addiction, your loved one, or you.

9. As in the case of suicide, one of the most important aids in your healing can come from finding something positive you can do in your loved one's honor. This may be small: talking to others with similar losses at support group meetings; writing notes, emails, or postings on social media. Later it might be larger: giving talks about your experiences and what you have learned about addiction and its effects to church, school, or civic groups. There is a public desire, and need, to learn from those with authentic experiences. You can do helpful, meaningful things your loved never had the opportunity to do.

What Others Should Not Do

Before proceeding to the suggestions dealing with how others might hinder or help, review the general dos and don'ts in chapter 4.

One of the most hurtful things to most bereaved people is being ghosted—abandoned by friends and acquaintances they felt they could depend on. They just disappear and stop communicating.

This applies especially to those whose loved ones died deaths stigmatized by others. If you just can't bring yourself to visit them in person right now, call them, write a note, contact them on social media. In whatever way you get in touch with them, once is not enough. Maintain contact. As soon as you can, try to see them in person.

If they tell you of some mean or inappropriate action the deceased did—verbal or physical abuse; lying; stealing money—maintain eye contact and listen but don't respond. A comment such as "What a loser" may seem supportive but usually does more harm than good. Don't add to their anger. They may need to tell this, but it is not a request for more negativity. Saying something such as "That must have hurt" or "That must have been hard to take" shows you understand the situation but doesn't add fuel to the fire.

What Others Can Do to Help

1. Be there. Because of the social stigma associated with addiction, many of the survivors tend to isolate themselves. They need someone who cares, someone who will listen to them without judging them. Be willing to continue to be there for a long time. Those who have lost loved ones to addiction tend to have fewer comforters than from most other causes.

2. Let them talk. A good way to start is to ask, "Do you want to talk about it?" You are there to listen, not to try to fix the unfixable. Listening is more helpful than talking. Let them talk about their loved one's addiction. Don't press for details. Let the bereaved take the lead. Let them discuss the good and the bad. While discussing the good, offer fond, amusing, or happy memories you have about the deceased.

3. Learn about addiction. Understand addiction is a disease. Let them know you understand this.

4. If you lost someone in your family to addiction, or someone in your family has a problem with addiction, it's okay to mention it. It helps them to know you have an idea what is going on with them. Even here, do not say, "I know just how you feel." You don't.

Closing Thought

As someone who has lost a son to one of these special circumstances, I remember how lonely, tiring, and painful it can be. You wonder, *Will I ever get through this? Will I ever enjoy life again?* This selection from Isaiah helped me:

> Have you not known? Have you not heard, the everlasting God, the Lord, the Creator of the ends of the earth, faints not, neither is weary? There is no searching of his understanding. He gives power to the faint and to them that have no might he increases strength. Even the youths shall faint and be weary, and the young men utterly fall: But they that wait on the Lord shall renew their strength; they shall mount up on wings like eagles; they shall run and not be weary; and they shall walk and not faint. (Isa. 40:28–31 NKJV)

In those dreadful early months of grief, I could barely crawl, much less walk. Finally, as I prayed and did my grief work, I could stagger a bit, then finally walk without fainting.

As I continued working, with the help of God and my Compassionate Friends, I could occasionally trot.

Now I can run and not be weary.

Sometimes I soar.

So can you.

6

Hold onto Your Faith

When someone dear to us dies, we embark on an uncharted grief journey. My goal in writing this book is to lend some guidance through this unfamiliar territory. I tried to keep personal references to a minimum. The ones I did use were to illustrate certain points. I wanted this to be a helpful guide, not a memoir.

This last part is purely personal.

My grief journey proceeded very much as I described it in the book. For the first two years, I floundered through confusion, disorganization, depression, anger, and guilt just like the rest of you. I rode the same roller coaster of emotions you did. Though sidetracked by two trials, I continued plowing through my grief work with my Compassionate Friends.

As I described in the poem "Turning Point," I really can't pinpoint a specific time when things began to change for the better. I just know somewhere in the six months after the second trial, it happened. My world became brighter. I began to look forward to living. About a year later, I reached acceptance, renewal, adaptation, or whatever I care to call it. I had come to terms with Brad's death. This journey will never be totally complete in this life. For now, my grief is like the metaphor of the cloud, just a small, distant, dark spot in an otherwise clear sky. I am at peace with this.

For many of us, the death of a loved one triggers a spiritual crisis, or at least a spiritual reassessment. In addition to our grief journey, we also find ourselves on a spiritual journey—a faith journey.

This is a brief account of my faith journey. I am not trying to preach a sermon. I mentioned earlier how sharing your story and experiences with your support group could help another member having similar problems. In the same way, I hope sharing my faith journey might benefit those of you with similar concerns as I had.

When a loved one dies, there is a real temptation to become lost in bitterness, blame and anger. In the thirty-five years I have worked with the bereaved, I have seen people become angry with and blame God. Some abandoned their faith completely.

I was not angry, nor did I blame Him. I was frustrated. I just felt I was not receiving the help and comfort the scriptures taught. I needed help. Where was God?

Where Is God in Grief?

In those early days of loss, grief, and mourning, when I was really hurting, where was God? As I was to find out, He was there all along but not always where I expected Him to be. So where did I find Him?

First, God is present is in Holy Scripture. I never read my Bible as desperately and as earnestly as in those first few months. I underlined in red everything that seemed to relate to my situation. Most of Job and a good portion of Psalms wound up in red. These gave me no clear-cut answers, but I still got some comfort from them. Here was a record of others, like Job and David, crying, ranting, and questioning just like me, and God stood by them. When I was not up to prolonged reading, I reread the underlined portions.

I found three selections to be particularly helpful and comforting. I copied them and pinned them to the corkboard above my computer screen. I read them repeatedly.

In the tumultuous early days of grief, it was easy for me to slide into self-pity and feel alone and abandoned by friends and acquaintances. Sometimes I was. It was a short step to including God among the abandoners. One day as I scanned my red underlines, I came across this verse: "God has said, 'Never will I leave you; never will I forsake you'" (Heb 13:5). Looking back, He never has.

I mentioned before, when you lose your parents, you lose your past. When you lose your child, you lose your future. I saw no hope for any future that lay ahead of me. Then I found one little scripture tucked away in Jeremiah:

> For I know the plans I have for you declares the
> Lord, plans to prosper you, not harm you, plans
> to give you hope and a future. (Jer 29:19)

The other was more familiar but just as helpful.

> For I am convinced that neither death nor life,
> neither angels nor demons, neither the present
> nor the future, nor any powers, neither height
> nor depth, nor anything else in all creation can
> separate us from the love of God that is in Christ
> Jesus our Lord. (Ro 8:38–39)

I found all three to be true. These were my daily touchstones as I ground forward through my grief.

The second place God was present was in my prayers. Prayer had never been my strong point, but in those painful early days of grief, I prayed as never before.

Much of the time, I didn't know what I needed, or what to pray for, or how to pray for it. I just hoped Paul was correct when he said the Spirit would intercede and pray for me.

I wasn't angry with God. I was frustrated. My whole life, I heard sermons and read scriptures assuring me of help and comfort in times of need.

> Yea, though I walk through the valley of the shadow of death, I will fear no evil; for You are with me; You rod and Your staff they comfort me. (Ps 23:4 NKJV)

I did not feel accompanied or comforted.

I remember three of my prayers particularly.

The first, I prayed during this time of annoyance, floundering, and frustration. I didn't feel God's presence. He seemed far away and hidden. One night, I knelt, and in the midst of praying, I shouted, "Where are You hiding? Come on out. Show Yourself. Speak to me." I got no answer. I didn't say this one again. I think I was afraid to repeat it.

The second prayer I repeated almost daily. One thing troubled me most. I was afraid the simplistic, unexamined faith I had lived my life by might be full of holes. I worried all the stuff I had claimed to believe might not be entirely true, or worse yet, was not true at all. I don't know how many times I prayed, "Just give me one sign that what I claim to believe is true, and it will all hang together." Not the prayer of a rock-solid believer, but it was honest, and it was mine.

In truth, God was there all the time. I was just so caught up in grief and frustration, and was complaining so loudly, I neither heard nor recognized Him.

Six weeks after Brad was killed, I was caring for my dad, who was in the late stages of ALS (Lou Gehrig's disease). Late one evening, my mother called and told me Dad couldn't swallow. We knew this was coming sooner or later. He had already told me, "No IVs or feeding tubes." I stopped on the way home from the hospital. The three of us talked about how Dad wanted us to proceed from this point. I shared none of the horrors of dehydration, starvation, and wasting I knew lay ahead.

When I got home, I said the third prayer. I prayed, "I know Dad is going to die, but please let him go quickly and don't let him hurt." Immediately after saying *amen*, the telephone rang. It was Mom. She said Dad had just stopped breathing.

All I could do was say, "Thank you. I don't need any more signs," and ask forgiveness for my petty need of a sign in the first place.

This wasn't an epiphany. It was as if God slapped me up aside my head and said, "Listen! I'm here. I'm not going away."

Some people have implied this answer to prayer imparted some glow of goodness on my part. I feel just the opposite. It was undeserved grace. Despite my frustration and doubts, God still answered my prayers for my dad, dispelled my misgivings, and restored my faith.

I was more like Thomas, to whom Jesus said, "Because you have seen me, you have believed; blessed are those who have not seen and yet have believed" (Jn 21:29). I think the message to me was "Because you have received a sign, you have believed; blessed are those who received no sign and yet have believed."

A third place God is present in our grief is through others. I am convinced we get glimpses of God in our neighbors' faces. The writer of Hebrews tells us we sometime meet angels without knowing it (Heb 13:2). I think this is true. Many people don't know what to say or do when someone dies and thus do nothing. Others do the best they can. I mentioned some things that help in chapter 3, but here are three that to me were God-sent.

My dad and Brad were best buddies. When Brad was killed, Dad was paralyzed from the neck down, and he was almost impossible to move. Two of my friends, unrequested and at their expense, hired an ambulance to take Dad to the funeral home to see his grandson one last time.

I had met the wife of another physician in town on two or three occasions. I considered her an acquaintance, not a close friend. She was a talented singer and musician. She wrote a beautiful song in memory of Brad, hired a band, and recorded it at a professional recording studio. I received the tape in the mail six weeks after his death. I received it on the very morning I was to take my mother to select a casket and make arrangements for Dad's funeral—the same procedure, at the same funeral home I had been to for Brad six weeks earlier. There is no way the tape and the timing could have been coincidences.

I think I was born to be a family doctor. My medical practice had been my life, and I loved it—until now. After Brad's death, I could no longer relate to my patients as I once did. What was I to do? I was miserable. I wrestled with this decision for more than a year. Out of nowhere, the hospital CEO asked me to meet with him. The hospital was beginning a hospitalist program, and he wanted me to direct it. I would have more time to spend with my wife and less emotional strain than in my private practice. This proved to be a God-given boost in my grief journey.

Sometimes God acts through others, and they don't even realize it.

My wife, Jean, was having a hard time staying in our home. It held too many memories. Our town was not large, and she was hesitant to go out and be recognized as "the murdered boy's mother." I prayed repeatedly, "Please do something to help Jean."

Our former pastor had retired and moved to a cabin he had personally built in the Smoky Mountains. He vowed he was going to stay there until he died. His two sons had staked claims to the cabin for when that occurred. We had had no contact for more than three years. Four months after Brad's death, out of the blue, he called and asked me if I was interested in buying his cabin. I was. This proved to be a primary source of Jean's healing. She spent three or four days every week in solitude away from our house, me, and other people, licking her wounds, hiking, and learning to cope with her loss. Why would my friend change his lifelong plans? Why would he think of us? What of his sons' claims? God knows—literally.

One profound way God helped me by means of people without their knowledge was through Brad's teachers. Brad was a talented writer. Because of this, he was always in honors English classes or their equivalent. His teachers required him to keep daily journals. He was so active with hunting, fishing, and sports he would never have done this on his own. His teachers forced him to. I had no idea he had written them. After his death, we found his journals from the ninth grade through his junior year in college scattered among his books, clothes, and hunting gear. I spent the next year reading them. I organized every entry and published them for family, friends, and teachers. I still read them several times a year. It is as if he's visiting me. His teachers have no idea their requirement for this writing exercise would, aside from my faith and The Compassionate Friends, do the most to preserve my will to live. Coincident? I think not.

Finally, God works through *us* in our grief. The Holy Spirit helps us do things we never dreamed we could do—things that, in turn, help us cope with and adapt to our losses. I had always read poetry, but I had never written anything but silly limericks. For some reason, I began writing poems after Brad died. Just getting my grief, pain, and memories on paper helped dispel some of my demons. I eventually published them. I have since sold more than five thousand copies and have several hundred letters from bereaved people all over the country telling how much the poems helped them. I am convinced these poems were God-sent. They came from beyond me.

As a sidenote, a great spur to our own healing is when we can help someone else with theirs. I think this is what Paul was referring to in his letter to the Corinthians.

> Praise be to the God and Father of our Lord Jesus Christ, the Father of compassion and the God of all comfort, who comforts us in all our troubles, so that we can comfort those in any trouble with the comfort we ourselves received from God. (2 Cor 1:3–4)

I am certain God is with us, perhaps is closest to us, in the midst of our pain, our suffering, our losses, and our grief.

So where is God in sorrow?

He is with us in Scripture, in our prayers, through the acts of others, in our own actions, and in ways we cannot begin to comprehend.

Faith

I said in the introduction I cannot separate the spiritual aspects (my faith) from the rest of my life. Neither can I separate my grief journey from my faith journey. I think my grief journey is as near over as it will ever be in this life. As I neared this point, my faith journey became more apparent. At times, I really sensed God's presence. My prayers turned more to gratitude for the obvious progress in coping with my grief. Even more, I prayed for guidance in where I should go with the rest of my life.

Prior to Brad's death, I lived my life following a faith molded by a lifetime of church attendance and traditional Protestant teaching. I had faith of a sort, but it was an unexamined faith.

I began to consider, *What is faith? What do I really believe?*

I had never given much thought to this. Through prayer and reflection, I have come to some ideas that ring true to me and have altered my life for the better. I offer them as a work in progress. I sometimes wander or become lazy. When I recognize it, I ask for forgiveness and try again. You might consider doing something similar.

These are my conclusions.

My faith at its core is three things and a corollary.

First, I believe God *is*. He is real, and His character is as described in Holy Scripture and as demonstrated in Jesus Christ.

Second, I believe God is active in us and our world. He will keep the promises He made in Holy Scripture.

Third, God is love. He loves all humanity, but He loves each of us individually; so much so He sent His son to die for us.

The corollary is this: out of gratitude, our faith impels us to acts of worship and of kindness, love, and service to others.

Arising from these core beliefs is the question, How can I learn to nurture, strengthen, and apply this faith? Three activities have been most helpful to me.

First is private and corporate Bible study. How better can I learn how I should live and what sort of person God would have me to be than through His Holy Word?

Second is an ongoing relationship with God sustained through prayer and introspection.

Third is being aware of God's workings in me and my world.

I have always been uneasy with attributing every single happening, no matter how small or trivial, to God's action. I don't believe I found a parking place near the door of Walmart yesterday because it was God's will. It was just a coincidence.

That said, I am convinced God works to bring us help, comfort, assurance, and, yes, even correction.

The answer to my prayer the night my dad died is the only occasion where I recognized God acting as it was happening.

I am, however, just as certain about God's actions in the tape arriving the morning after Dad's death, the new medical practice, the house for Jean, and Brad's journals. But these I recognized in retrospect. I'm sure He acted many more times I missed or have forgotten.

The event with my dad was a heavenly thunderbolt. The only one I have ever seen.

Others were gentle nudges from God. I think all our "random acts of kindness" are nudges from God. They benefit both the recipient and the doer. Nudges softly saying to the recipients, "I'm here, I care, I won't leave you alone." To the doers, he whispers, "Well done."

Journey's End

Many of you are reading this book because, like me, you are on a grief journey. I hope, in time, you can come to terms with your loss. I hope you, too, are on a faith journey. The two go hand in hand and complement each other.

Our grief journey will end when we end. What then? Our faith journey continues for eternity.

I have always viewed conception and death as points on a continuum.

An embryo in the uterus is not insensate. In fact, it becomes more sensate as it develops. It feels pain and withdraws from a pinprick. It is startled by sudden jolts or noises. Its vision, taste buds, and sense of smell are functional at birth. At a rudimentary level, it must have some sense of something out there beyond itself. At birth, it is thrust into an environment it was incapable of conceiving beforehand.

I see death as a door to another dimension—a dimension of which we have little better concept than that newborn baby had of the world of sight, sound, and people into which it emerged.

What do we know about this next dimension?

We know it exists. Jesus assures us it does.

> My Father's house has many rooms; if that were not so, would I have told you that I am going there to prepare a place for you? And if I go and prepare a place for you, I will come back and take you to be with me that you also may be where I am. (Jn 14:2–3)

Through near-death experiences, we have hints of some of its nature. We call it heaven. What will this place, heaven, be like?

I believe I will see Brad again, but I have no idea what that reunion will be like. Many people think heaven will be a continuation of our present existence with the bad parts removed. My mother was convinced Brad and Dad were fishing together in heaven. This may be so, but everything I know about God says heaven will be more, far more, and it will all be good.

I choose to agree with Paul and, until the time comes, let it go at that.

> Eye has not seen, nor ear heard,
> Nor have entered the heart of man
> The things which God has prepared for those
> who love Him. (1 Cor 2:9 NKJV)

Godspeed on both your grief and faith journeys. Cling to the memories of your loved one. Strive to bring meaning to their life and yours. Hold onto your faith.

I leave you with this parting thought.

We are told in Hebrews, "Let us hold unswervingly to the hope we possess, for he who promised is faithful" (Heb 10:23).

What has He promised to those who mourn? *They will be comforted.* God has plans to give them *hope and a future.* But He has promised more than that. He said, "'God himself will be with them and be their God. He will wipe every tear from their eyes. There will be no more death or mourning or crying or pain, for the old order of things has passed away.' He who was seated on the throne said, 'I am making everything new!' Then he said, 'Write this down, for the words are trustworthy and true'" (Rev 21:4–5).

Amen.